Level
3-A

AIM HIGH 에임하이
READING 리딩

In-Depth Lab

We're
위아북스

AIM HIGH READING   Level 3-A

지은이	In-Depth Lab	주소	서울특별시 종로구 인사동 194 홍익빌딩 4층
펴낸이	전수용 · 조상현	TEL	02-725-9988 FAX 02-725-9863
기획책임	최상호	디자인	플랜필드
펴낸곳	(주)위아북스	제작	정민문화사
등록번호	제 300-2007-164호	출력	우성 C&P

ISBN 978-89-93258-11-0
ISBN 978-89-93258-10-3 (세트)

www.wearebooks.co.kr

Level
3-A

AIM HIGH 에임하이
READING 리딩

In-Depth Lab

We're
위아북스

PROLOGUE

독해(Reading Comprehension)는 모든 학업의 기초로서 이제는 글을 읽고 이해하는 능력만을 평가하는 것에 그치지 않고, 독해한 내용을 바탕으로 말하기, 쓰기는 물론 청취한 내용과 함께 통합 학습 능력을 평가하는 데 있어 꼭 필요한 능력이 되었다. 독해를 하는 데 가장 어려움을 호소하는 부분은 어휘라고 생각하는 사람들이 많다. 물론 어휘력은 영어의 기초라고 할 수 있다. 하지만 단어는 아는데, 해석이 안 되고, 전체 문장을 이해하지 못하는 경우들이 많다. 문장들은 이해했으나 글의 흐름을 파악하지 못하여 전체적인 글을 이해하지 못하는 경우 또한 많다.

따라서 본 교재는 글의 기본적인 세부 내용을 이해하고, 나아가 문장의 흐름 및 일관성(Coherence), 전체적인 이해를 묻는 요약(Summary), 주제(Main Idea), 어법(Grammar), 어휘(Vocabulary) 등 다양한 독해 기술을 훈련할 수 있는 문제들을 포함하고 있다. 이런 문제들을 통해 단순히 어휘의 의미를 나열하여 해석하는 수준에서 나아가, 주어진 글을 이해하고 난 후에 세부적인 문장들의 구조를 해부하여 면밀히 살펴봄으로써 글을 세부적, 전체적으로 이해하는 수준까지 끌어올릴 수 있게 구성되어 있다.

또한 독해 능력을 향상시키기 위해 영어의 구조와 영어식 표현 방법을 이해하는 데 초점이 맞추어져 있다. 지문과 문제 풀이가 끝나면 Grammar와 Structure라는 코너를 통해 문장의 주요 구조를 충분히 숙지하고, 필요한 문법을 연습할 수 있다. Writing이라는 코너에서는 말이 어떻게 전개되는지를 파악하는 훈련이 되도록 하였다. 이와 같은 장치들을 통한 지속적인 독해 훈련으로 영어에서는 말을 어떻게 구성하는지, 어떤 단위로 생각을 정리해 가는지를 읽을 수 있는 것이다. 이런 장치들을 통해 영어 문장들의 구조가 자연스럽게 파악되고 문장 및 글의 독해력이 향상될 수 있다.

최근 특목고 입시, 텝스, 토플 등의 영어 시험들을 살펴보면, 교과서에서 만나는 지문이라기보다 실질적으로 영어 환경에서 많이 접하게 되는 뉴스, 광고, 기사, 공지 등과 같은 현실적인 지문들을 다루고 있다는 것을 볼 수 있다. 꼭 시험 때문이 아니더라도, 실질적으로 필요한 독해를 위해서 이러한 지문들을 많이 접하는 것은 좋은 훈련이 될 것이다. 따라서 본 교재는 학문적인 지문을 포함하여, 뉴스, 기사, 공지, 광고 등의 다양한 지문 유형을 다뤘으며, 과학, 건강, 역사, 상식 등의 다양한 주제를 담고 있다.

또한 독해의 길이가 점점 길어지는 추세에 따라 한 가지 주제를 가진 긴 글을 빨리 읽고 이해하는 훈련을 위해, 지문의 길이를 실제 특목고 입시나 텝스보다도 길게 하여 빠르면서도 정확한 내용 이해를 연습하도록 하였다.

어휘나 해석 때문에 영문 독해를 만나면 답답하고 두려웠던 부분들을 떨쳐버리고 다음 내용이 궁금해지고 글을 읽으면 읽을 수록 재미를 느낄 수 있는 단계까지 도달하기를 희망한다.

In-Depth Lab

■ 구성 ■

Level 1-A · B

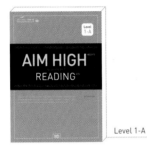

Level 1-A

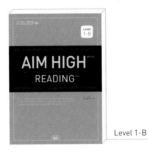

Level 1-B

- 지문 수 _ 40 (A: 20 / B: 20)
- 지문별 글자 수 _ 150~200
- 특징 _ 정보 스캔 및 글의 흐름 파악 문제 다수

Level 2-A · B

Level 2-A

Level 2-B

- 지문 수 _ 40 (A: 20 / B: 20)
- 지문별 글자 수 _ 170~220
- 특징 _ 세부 사항 및 어법 문제 다수

Level 3-A · B

Level 3-A

Level 3-B

- 지문 수 _ 40 (A: 20 / B: 20)
- 지문별 글자 수 _ 200~250
- 특징 _ 정보 스캔 및 분석 문제 다수

■ 특장점 ■

1 실질적인 지문과 다양한 주제 Authentic and Various Topics

신문, 잡지, 인터넷 등에서 실질적으로 많이 접해야 하는 소재와 내용의 지문들을 엄선하였다. 그리고 과학, 기술, 역사 등의 학문적인 내용에서 정보, 생활, 문화, 경제 등의 다양한 주제를 다루었다.

2 독해력 향상을 위한 9가지 문제 형식 Questions for Reading Skill Building

외형적인 문제의 분류가 아닌, 독해 기술 향상을 위한 Reading Skill을 9가지로 분류하여 다양한 문제 형태를 통해 독해력을 기를 수 있도록 문제를 고안하였다.

■ 9 Reading Skill Building Question Types
⋯ Info Scan, Analysis, Summary, Reference, Inference, Detail, Vocabulary, Coherence, Grammar

3 독해력과 직결된 9가지 핵심 문법 정리 Grammar for Reading

독해에 필요한 또는 독해를 어렵게 하는 문법들을 분류하여 각 지문별로 지문의 내용을 파악 다음 독해 속의 문법을 학습할 수 있도록 배치하였다.

■ 9 Grammar Points
⋯ 부정사/동명사, 시제, 관계사/절, 가정법, 동사/조동사, 명사/대명사, 분사/수동태, 형용사/부사/비교, 기타

4 독해력을 위한 8가지 핵심 구조 파악 Structure for Reading

문장 구조에서 독해를 어렵게 하는 전형적인 8가지의 형태를 분류하여 중점적으로 학습할 수 있도록 각 지문별로 배치하였다. 특히 명사가 형용사절, 분사구, 전치사구의 수식을 받을 경우 이해의 흐름이 끊길 수 있다는 점에서 이 부분을 집중적으로 학습하도록 하였다.

■ 8 Structure Types
⋯ 형용사절의 명사 수식, to부정사, 명사절, 전치사구의 명사 수식, 부사절의 명사 수식, 분사의 명사 수식, 동사, 복합 부사구

5 독해 지문을 활용한 영작 Writing for Reading

지문에서 다루었던 핵심적인 문법이나, 구조를 영작을 통해 복습하도록 하여, 영작 및 어휘, 문법, 구조를 확실히 학습하도록 하였다.

■ Level 별 Topics ■

	Level	Passage #	
Life / Sport / Music	Level 1	12	
	Level 2	14	
	Level 3	8	
Science / Technology / Nature	Level 1	7	
	Level 2	6	
	Level 3	18	
Social / Culture / Business	Level 1	13	
	Level 2	10	
	Level 3	6	
Food / Health	Level 1	8	
	Level 2	6	
	Level 3	2	
Person / History	Level 1	0	
	Level 2	4	
	Level 3	6	

■ Level 별 Reading Skill Building Question Types ■

	Level	Passage #	
Info Scan	Level 1	30	
	Level 2	27	
	Level 3	36	
Analysis	Level 1	28	
	Level 2	27	
	Level 3	46	
Summary	Level 1	6	
	Level 2	6	
	Level 3	5	
Reference	Level 1	11	
	Level 2	8	
	Level 3	5	
Inference	Level 1	9	
	Level 2	11	
	Level 3	12	
Detail	Level 1	9	
	Level 2	21	
	Level 3	13	
Vocabulary	Level 1	8	
	Level 2	11	
	Level 3	21	
Coherence	Level 1	30	
	Level 2	21	
	Level 3	21	
Grammar	Level 1	12	
	Level 2	28	
	Level 3	1	

■ Level별 Grammar Points ■

	Level	Passage #	
부정사 / 동명사	Level 1	6	
	Level 2	6	
	Level 3	7	
시제	Level 1	1	
	Level 2	4	
	Level 3	4	
관계대명사와 절	Level 1	5	
	Level 2	7	
	Level 3	6	
가정법	Level 1	2	
	Level 2	1	
	Level 3	2	
동사 / 조동사	Level 1	7	
	Level 2	8	
	Level 3	6	
명사 / 대명사	Level 1	2	
	Level 2	3	
	Level 3	2	
분사 / 수동태	Level 1	2	
	Level 2	3	
	Level 3	2	
형용사 / 부사 / 비교	Level 1	6	
	Level 2	5	
	Level 3	3	
기타	Level 1	9	
	Level 2	3	
	Level 3	8	

■ Level별 Structure Types ■

	Level	Passage #	
형용사절의 명사 수식	Level 1	12	
	Level 2	13	
	Level 3	10	
to부정사의 다양한 용법	Level 1	5	
	Level 2	5	
	Level 3	3	
what, if 등이 이끄는 명사절	Level 1	5	
	Level 2	5	
	Level 3	5	
전치사구의 수식을 받는 (동)명사구	Level 1	8	
	Level 2	8	
	Level 3	4	
분사구의 명사 수식	Level 1	4	
	Level 2	8	
	Level 3	7	
동격 / 삽입 / 생략 / 병렬	Level 1	0	
	Level 2	0	
	Level 3	7	
4·5형식 문장	Level 1	2	
	Level 2	0	
	Level 3	0	
복합 부사구	Level 1	3	
	Level 2	0	
	Level 3	1	

AIM HIGH READING _ Level 3 구성 분석

Topics

⠿ Reading Skill Building Question Types

Reading Skills	문제수
Info Scan	36
Analysis	46
Summary	5
Reference	5
Inference	12
Detail	13
Vocabulary	21
Coherence	21
Grammar	1

Info Scan

지문 전체의 정보를 훑어보고, 주어진 선택지의 설명이 옳은지를 파악하는 능력을 연습한다.
• 지문을 전체적으로 이해하는 훈련이 된다.　• 빠른 독해를 할 수 있는 훈련이 된다.

Analysis

정보와 정보 사이의 유기적인 관계를 이해하는 연습을 한다. 시문의 특성한 한 곳에서 뿐
아니라, 여러 곳의 정보를 이해하고 이를 분석하여 이해하는 연습을 한다.
• 분석력을 향상시킨다.　• 논리력을 향상시킨다.

Summary

세부적인 사항의 이해가 아니라, 전체 글 또는 단락의 글을 이해하고 종합적으로 요약,
정리하는 능력을 연습한다.
• 논리력을 향상시킨다.　• 긴 글의 요약 및 정리 능력을 향상시킨다.

Reference

지시어가 가리키는 단어 또는 생각을 파악하는 능력을 연습한다.
• 정보 간의 관계를 파악하는 능력을 향상시킨다.
• 여러 다양한 표현을 사용하는 영어 지문의 독해력을 향상시킨다.

Inference

주어진 정보를 토대로 유추하고 추론하는 능력을 향상시킨다. 주제나 제목의 추론, 저자의 의도
추론은 물론, 주어진 정보에서, 나아가 단락 또는 지문을 통해 추론하는 능력을 연습한다.
• 주제, 제목, 저자의 의도를 추론하는 능력을 향상시킨다.
• 짧은 정보, 단락 또는 전체 글에서 추론하는 능력을 향상시킨다.

Detail

지문에서 세부적인 정보의 위치를 파악하고, 그 내용을 이해하는 연습을 한다.
• 세부 내용의 이해력을 향상시킨다.　• 영어로 주어지는 정보의 이해력을 향상시킨다.

Vocabulary

기본 어휘 능력과 문맥을 통해 어휘를 의미를 파악하는 연습을 한다.
• 기본 어휘력을 향상시킨다.　• 문맥상의 어휘 의미를 찾는 능력을 향상시킨다.

Coherence

글 또는 생각의 흐름상 자연스러운 내용이나, 앞뒤 정보간의 관계를 파악하는 연습을 한다.
• 단락의 주제문 또는 요약문을 찾는 능력을 향상시킨다.
• 정보 간의 관계를 빠르게 이해하는 능력을 향상시킨다.

Grammar

독해에서 가장 많이 쓰이고, 글을 이해하는 가장 필요한 문법 사항들을 연습한다.
• 문장의 이해력을 향상시킨다.　• 직독·직해 능력을 향상시킨다.

∵ Grammar Points

Structure Types

Structure	Passage No.	Sentence
형용사절의 명사 수식	02	Some Neanderthals who inhabited Europe and Central Asia
	04	The flight operation system that they had been working with
	07	Aqueducts that carried water into Roman cities
	14	salicylic acid which came from the bark of the willow tree
	15	a few tens of thousands of years, which is not a long time
	16	bee colonies in which the bees have been disappearing
	22	the world's population that is experiencing adolescence
	29	visual stimuli which are processed by the right hemisphere
	34	the dragon which in Asian tradition is admired
	39	the flat board furniture his father had been creating
	40	like the one that is used for broom handles
to부정사의 다양한 용법	08	engineered by scientists to produce protein drugs
	09	something called an electron gun to push electrons
	28	started using satellite imagery to solve the problem
what/if/whether/how가 이끄는 명사절	05	What all bats have in common is
	10	What has always perplexed researchers is
	31	What happens near Laurel Island is
	35	we are telling it exactly what we want it to do
	36	results in what might be considered a type
전치사구의 수식을 받는 (동)명사구	12	A few, such as Pan, Atlas, Prometheus, and Pandora,
	24	The process of breaking down skin oil before turning into acne
	26	The students' self-esteem as well as their attitudes
	33	20 of 5 to 6-year-olds from wealthy, well-educated families
분사구의 명사 수식	06	The "associations" started by his followers
	13	The person falling into a hypnotic trance
	18	Patients suffering from bipolar II disorder
	20	The pulses generated by the electrically excitable membrane
	21	A vine native to Asia called Oriental Bittersweet
	27	The sulfur dioxide emitted from the smokestacks
	37	nuisances brought on by anti-social neighbours
동격 / 삽입 / 생략 / 병렬	01	incredibly hot, about 6,000 Kelvin, but not so hot
	11	two or three different, seemingly unrelated stories
	19	The revelation that one American cow had mad cow disease
	23	The fact that the different manifestations of our reality
	25	which have proven without a doubt that the block is
	30	The worker bees, all sterile females, usually work to death
	32	four terrestrial or rocky inner planets and four gas giant outer planets
복합 부사구	03	such as the size and composition as well as the reflective properties
분사구문	38	Stressed by unsympathetic bosses, we feel on edge.
관계부사절	17	United States, where they often occupy the same territory

AIM HIGH READING _ Level 3 구성 및 특징

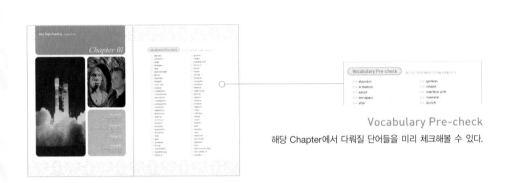

Vocabulary Pre-check

해당 Chapter에서 다뤄질 단어들을 미리 체크해볼 수 있다.

지문

신문, 잡지, 인터넷 등에서 실질적으로 많이 접해야 하는 소재와 내용의 지문들을 엄선하였다. 그리고 과학, 기술, 역사 등의 학문적인 내용에서 정보, 생활, 문화, 경제 등의 다양한 주제를 다뤘다.

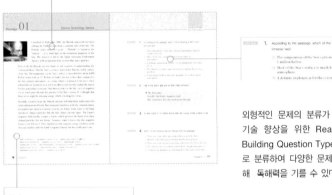

문제

외형적인 문제의 분류가 아닌, 독해 기술 향상을 위한 Reading Skill Building Question Types을 9가지로 분류하여 다양한 문제 형태를 통해 독해력을 기를 수 있다.

Words

본문에 쓰인 어휘들을 제시함으로써, 단어가 독해의 흐름을 끊지 않도록 되어 있다. 선행학습이 가능하다.

Grammar

독해에 필요한 또는 독해를 어렵게
하는 문법들을 분류하여 각 지문별
로 지문의 내용을 파악, 다음 독해
속의 문법을 학습할 수 있다.

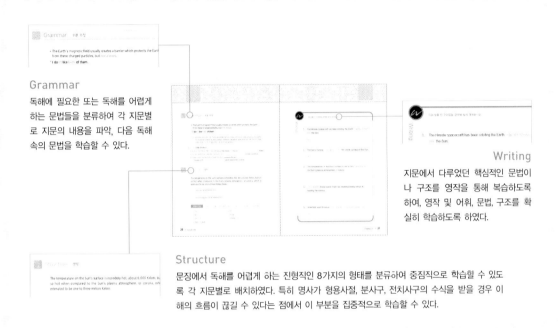

Writing

지문에서 다루었던 핵심적인 문법이
나 구조를 영작을 통해 복습하도록
하여, 영작 및 어휘, 문법, 구조를 확
실히 학습하도록 하였다.

Structure

문장에서 독해를 어렵게 하는 진형적인 8가지의 형태를 분류하여 중점적으로 학습할 수 있도
록 각 지문별로 배치하였다. 특히 명사가 형용사절, 분사구, 전치사구의 수식을 받을 경우 이
해의 흐름이 끊길 수 있다는 점에서 이 부분을 집중적으로 학습할 수 있다.

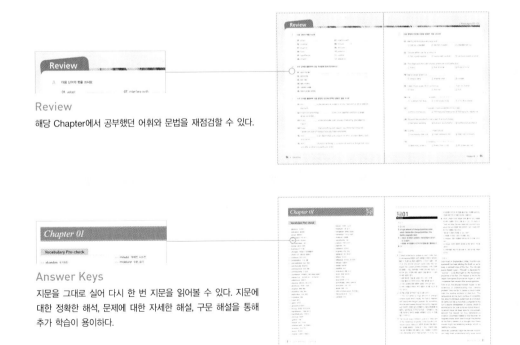

Review

해당 Chapter에서 공부했던 어휘와 문법을 재점검할 수 있다.

Answer Keys

지문을 그대로 실어 다시 한 번 지문을 읽어볼 수 있다. 지문에
대한 정확한 해석, 문제에 대한 자세한 해설, 구문 해설을 통해
추가 학습이 용이하다.

CONTENTS

Chapter 01

▨▨ abandon
▨▨ activation
▨▨ adopt
▨▨ aerospace
▨▨ alter
▨▨ approximately
▨▨ barrier
▨▨ byproduct
▨▨ charged
▨▨ churn out
▨▨ coalesce
▨▨ composition
▨▨ concentration
▨▨ conclusively
▨▨ consequence
▨▨ consequently
▨▨ counteract
▨▨ depend on
▨▨ determiner
▨▨ disperse
▨▨ enormous
▨▨ eruption
▨▨ exception
▨▨ exploration
▨▨ formation
▨▨ fossil
▨▨ gene
▨▨ grassland
▨▨ hiccup
▨▨ hypothesize
▨▨ hypothetically
▨▨ identical

▨▨ ignition
▨▨ inhabit
▨▨ interfere with
▨▨ inversion
▨▨ launch
▨▨ master
▨▨ minute *a.*
▨▨ moisture
▨▨ navigation
▨▨ numerous
▨▨ obstacle
▨▨ opportunity
▨▨ particle
▨▨ pigment
▨▨ preserve
▨▨ property
▨▨ radiation
▨▨ reflect
▨▨ reflective
▨▨ release
▨▨ reveal
▨▨ satellite
▨▨ seed
▨▨ sequence
▨▨ skull
▨▨ spacecraft
▨▨ specifically
▨▨ specimen
▨▨ stock
▨▨ telecommunication
▨▨ the number of
▨▨ variable *n.*

Launched in September 2006, the Hinode spacecraft has been orbiting the Earth so as to keep a constant view of the Sun. The Hinode space mission's goal — "Hinode" is Japanese for "sunrise" — is to shed light on the mysterious properties of the Sun. The mission is led by the Japan Aerospace Exploration Agency, with cooperation from several other space agencies.

First of all, the Hinode mission hopes to aid scientists in understanding the "corona problem," that the Sun's corona is much hotter than the visible surface of the Sun. The temperature on the Sun's surface is incredibly hot, about 6,000 Kelvin (water boils at 373 Kelvin on Earth), but not so hot when compared to the Sun's plasma atmosphere, or corona, which is estimated to be one to three million Kelvin. Scientists have not been able to conclusively explain the reason for this temperature inversion. One theory relates to the discovery of magnetic waves which pass through the plasma of the Sun's corona. It is thought that these waves might be releasing energy which is heating the corona.

Secondly, scientists hope the Hinode mission will help them understand why solar wind generated by the Sun sometimes interferes with telecommunications, navigation and electrical power systems on Earth. Solar wind is the huge amount of charged particles that the Sun churns out into space. The Earth's magnetic field usually creates a barrier which protects the Earth from these charged particles, but not always. Scientists want to know why this magnetic barrier is not full-proof. They hypothesize that magnetic energy eruptions on the Sun may interfere with the Earth's magnetic barrier, but they really aren't sure.

Words

- shed [ʃed] (빛을) 퍼뜨리다 • aerospace [ɛ́ərouspèis] 우주 공간 • plasma [plǽzmə] 플라스마, 전리(電離) 기체
- Kelvin [kélvin] 켈빈(절대온도 단위) • inversion [invə́:rʒən] 반대, 역적 • pass through ~을 통과하다
- interfere with ~을 방해하다 • telecommunication [teləkəmjù:nəkéiʃən] 원거리통신 • charged [tʃɑ:rdʒd] 전하를 띤, 대전(帶電)한
- particle [pá:rtikl] 미립자, 분자 • churn out 대량으로 발생하다 • barrier [bǽriər] 울타리, 장벽
- hypothesize [haipáθəsàiz] 가설을 세우다 • eruption [irʌ́pʃən] 분출, 폭발

1. According to the passage, which of the following is NOT true? (choose two)

    ① The temperature of the Sun's plasma atmosphere exceeds 1 million Kelvin.

    ② Most of the Sun's surface is much hotter than its atmosphere.

    ③ A definite explanation for the corona problem has not been given.

    ④ The Hinode brought some data that can explain the corona problem.

    ⑤ Some people believe the Sun's magnetic waves heat up its atmosphere.

2. 다음 빈칸에 알맞은 말을 넣어 세 번째 단락을 요약하시오.

    ➜ The Sun emits ....

      Usually, the Earth's magnetic field ....

      But, sometimes, the solar wind passes through

      ....

3. 이 글에 언급된 두 가지 태양의 특성과 이에 대한 Hinode 미션을 우리말로 쓰시오.

    • .... : ....

    • .... : ....

4. Which of the following can be inferred from the passage?

    ① There are some other spaceships that research the Sun.

    ② Hinode is the first spacecraft launched by the Japanese.

    ③ There are some theories regarding unknown facts about the Sun.

    ④ The Hinode mission will last until it finds enough information.

    ⑤ Scientists are planning another launch for the study of the Sun.

Grammar   부분 부정

- The Earth's magnetic field usually creates a barrier which protects the Earth from these charged particles, but not always.

+ I don't like both of them.

Tips 일반적으로 쓰이는 완전 부정 구문과는 달리 문장을 부분적으로 부정하는 경우가 있다. 이것을 부분 부정이라 한다. 일반적으로 부정어(not, never)가 all, every, always, necessary, altogether, quite, both 등과 함께 쓰여 부분 부정을 이룬다. '전체가 ~는 아니다, 혹은 거의가 ~은 아니다' 라고 해석한다.

❙ Quiz 다음을 영작하시오.

1. 당신이 비난을 전적으로 면할 수는 있는 것은 아니다. (free, entirely) → You're _____ blame.

2. 모든 책이 재미를 주거나 이득을 주는 것은 아니다. → _____ interest or profit us.

3. 인생에서 성공은 부의 획득과 반드시 동일한 것은 아니다. (necessarily, the same)
   → Success in life _____ as the acquirement of riches.

Structure   생략

The temperature on the Sun's surface is incredibly hot, about 6,000 Kelvin, but not so hot when compared to the Sun's plasma atmosphere, or corona, which is estimated to be one to three million Kelvin.

◎ not so hot 앞에 생략되었을 말은?

   → ....

◎ when과 compared 사이에 생략되었을 말은?

   → ....

문장의 구조	주어 + 동사 + 보어, but + 보어 + (부사절) + (관계사절)

- 주어 → ....
- 동사 → ....
- 보어 → ....
- 연결어 → but

- 보어 → ....
- (부사절) → ....
- (관계사절) → ....

Writing

다음 밑줄 친 우리말을 문맥에 맞게 영작하시오.

1. The Hinode spacecraft has been orbiting the Earth ~을 계속 지켜보기 위해 the Sun.

   └→

2. The Sun's corona ~보다 훨씬 더 뜨겁다 the visible surface of the Sun.

   └→

3. The temperature on the Sun's surface is not so hot ~와 비교할 때 the Sun's plasma atmosphere, or corona.

   └→

4. ~라고 생각된다 these waves might be releasing energy which is heating the corona.

   └→

5. Scientists want to know 이 자기장 방벽이 완전히 막아내지 못하는 이유.

   └→

Have you ever seen a picture of a Neanderthal caveman with red hair and pale skin? Probably not. But a European research team has found that hypothetically speaking some Neanderthals who inhabited Europe and Central Asia approximately 230,000 to 30,000 years ago could have had such hair color as well as light skin. Since the actual hair and skin of Neanderthals have not been preserved, all the knowledge we have of Neanderthals comes from examining fossils such as skull bones.

(A) Carles Lalueza, a professor of the University of Barcelona, and some assistant researchers studied DNA samples from Neanderthal fossils. (B) They looked specifically at the sequence of the MC1R gene. (C) In modern humans of European stock, this gene is responsible for pale skin and red hair since this DNA sequence directs cells to produce the pigment melanin which is the primary determiner of hair and skin color in humans. (D)

The research, however, revealed that this gene and the one in modern humans are not identical. (E) Wanting to find out how this Neanderthal gene affected melanin production, they conducted further tests. They inserted the Neanderthal gene into cells that were growing in a test tube. The results showed that even though the Neanderthal MC1R gene and the modern human MC1R gene were different, they had the same effect on the production of melanin. Consequently, the researchers conclude that it is possible that there were red-haired and fair-skinned Neanderthals.

Words _____

- **Neanderthal** [niǽndərθɑ̀:l] 네안데르탈인(人)의 · **hypothetically** [hàipəθétikəli] 가정하여 · **preserve** [prizə́:rv] 보존하다
- **skull** [skʌl] 두개골 · **specifically** [spisífikəli] 정확하게 · **sequence** [síːkwəns] 배열, 순서 · **stock** [stɑk] 혈통, 가계
- **pigment** [pígmənt] 색소 · **melanin** [mélənin] 멜라닌 · **determiner** [ditə́:rminər] 결정인자
- **consequently** [kánsikwəntli] 결과적으로 · **specimen** [spésəmən] 표본, 견본

Info Scan **1.** According to the passage, which of the following is NOT correct?

① Scientists have studied the hair and skin attached to Neanderthal fossils.

② The sequence of the MC1R gene is what decides hair and skin color in humans.

③ The MC1R sequence of modern humans is different than that of Neanderthals.

④ It is the MC1R gene that commands cells to produce melanin in humans.

⑤ Discovered fossils of Neanderthals have been the only source of information.

Analysis **2.** 네안데르탈인에 대한 실험의 결과와 이를 통한 결론을 우리말로 쓰시오.

• 결과: ....

• 결론: ....

Vocabulary **3.** 밑줄 친 identical과 바꾸어 쓸 수 있는 말은?

① discernible　　② alike　　③ different
④ separated　　⑤ distinguishable

Coherence **4.** (A)~(E) 중, 글의 흐름상 주어진 문장이 들어가기 가장 적절한 곳은?

The researchers analyzed DNA samples from two Neanderthal specimens from Spain and Italy.

① (A)　　② (B)　　③ (C)
④ (D)　　⑤ (E)

Grammar 병렬구조

- There were red-haired and fair-skinned Neanderthals.
+ She is very young and extremely intelligent.
+ The population of Korea is smaller than that of Japan.

Tips 접속사나 comma에 의해 단어, 구나 절이 연결될 때, 혹은 비교구문에서 비교의 대상이 되는 내용들끼리는 동일 범주의
문법 구조 및 동일 범주의 내용을 병치해야 한다.

▌Quiz 다음 문장에서 매끄럽지 못한 부분을 고쳐 다시 쓰시오.

1. She is not a musician but writes novels.

→ _____

2. I would like both free time and to be given extra money.

→ _____

3. We found the hotel very convenient and was not too expensive.

→ _____

Structure 형용사절의 명사 수식

Some Neanderthals who inhabited Europe and Central Asia approximately 230,000
to 30,000 years ago could have had such hair color as well as light skin.

◎ Some Neanderthals란 어떤 사람들인가?

→ _____

문장의 구조	주어 + 동사 + 목적어

- 주어 → ....
- 동사 → ....
- 목적어 → ....

Writing

다음 밑줄 친 우리말을 문맥에 맞게 영작하시오.

1. But a European research team has found that hypothetically speaking some Neanderthals 그런 머리색을 가지고 있었을 수도 있다 as well as light skin.

    └→
    ....

2. All the knowledge we have of Neanderthals 화석을 조사한 것에서 나온다 such as skull bones.

    └→
    ....

3. This DNA sequence 세포로 하여금 ~을 생성하라고 지시하다 the pigment melanin which is the primary determiner of hair and skin color in humans.

    └→
    ....

4. The research, however, revealed that this gene and the one in modern humans 동일하지 않다.

    └→
    ....

5. The researchers conclude that it is possible that there were 빨간 머리 카락에 하얀 피부의 네안데르탈인들.

    └→
    ....

Aerosols, which are minute particles in the air, are produced naturally and by human actions. Aerosols are a natural byproduct of chemical processes occurring in volcanoes, dust storms, sea spray, grassland fires and a host of other natural activities. Numerous human actions which can be in fact copies of natural actions thus also create aerosols.

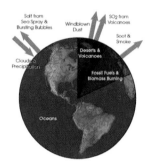

Aerosols have the effect of cooling the Earth's surface since they reflect light from the sun back into space. When this occurs, less solar radiation warms the Earth's surface. The degree to which the Earth is cooled depends on many variables, such as the size and composition of the particles, as well as the reflective properties of the materials on the Earth's surface immediately below the aerosols. Scientists are wondering if the cooling effect of aerosols will counteract the greenhouse effect which has been warming the Earth's surface for the last few decades.

(A) Aerosols are also thought to indirectly influence the climate of the Earth by altering the composition of clouds. (B) In fact, without aerosols in the atmosphere, there would be no clouds. Minute aerosol particles are the "seeds" which begin the process of the formation of cloud droplets. (C) As the number of aerosol particles increases inside a cloud, the moisture in that cloud disperses into each aerosol particle thus reducing the concentration of water in each particle. (D) This has two consequences — clouds with smaller drops reflect more sunlight, and such clouds last longer, because it takes more time for small drops to coalesce into drops that are large enough to fall to the ground. (E)

Words

• aerosol [ɛ́ərəsɔ̀:l] 【물리·화학】 에어로졸 • minute [mainjú:t] 미세한, 사소한 • particle [pɑ́:rtikl] 분자
• byproduct [baiprɑ́dəkt] 부산물 • grassland [grǽslænd] 목초지 • a host of 많은 ~ • radiation [rèidiéiʃən] 복사 에너지
• variable [vɛ́əriəbəl] 변수 • counteract [kàuntərǽkt] (효과 등을) 없애다 • alter [ɔ́:ltər] 바꾸다, 변경하다 • moisture [mɔ́istʃər] 수분, 습기
• disperse [dispə́:rs] 흩뜨리다 • concentration [kὰnsəntréiʃən] 농도, 집중 • coalesce [kòuəlés] 응집시키다

Info Scan **1.** According to the passage, which of the following is true?

① Aerosols result in human activities that are similar to nature.
② Aerosols are one of the main causes for global warming.
③ Aerosols reflect most of the harmful sunlight back to space.
④ Aerosols can be created from many different Earth activities.
⑤ Aerosols can lower the Earth's temperature to a dangerous level.

Analysis **2.** aerosol이 만드는 구름의 영향을 우리말로 설명하시오.

• 영향 1: ....

• 영향 2: ....

Detail **3.** 과학자들이 aerosols에 관심을 갖는 이유를 우리말로 쓰시오.

....

Coherence **4.** (A)~(E) 중, 다음 주어진 문장이 들어가기에 가장 적절한 곳은?

Both the effects increase the amount of sunlight that is reflected into space without reaching the surface.

① (A)   ② (B)   ③ (C)
④ (D)   ⑤ (E)

Grammar　가정법 과거 대용

- In fact, without aerosols in the atmosphere, there *would be* no clouds.

+ Without your help, I *could* not *succeed*.
  = But for your help, I *could* not *succeed*.
  = If it were not for your help, I *could* not *succeed*.

Tips 일반적으로 가정법 문장은 접속사 if가 이끄는 조건절과 귀결절로 이루어져 있는데, 조건절을 대신하는 표현들이 있다.

| Quiz　다음을 영작하시오.

1. 중력이 없다면, 사과는 땅에 떨어지지 않을 것이다. (gravity, without)
   → ＿＿＿＿＿＿＿＿＿＿＿＿＿＿＿, an apple would not fall to the ground.

2. 그 기술이 아니었다면, 그 학습경험이 유용할 수 있을까? (but)
   → Would the learning experience be available ＿＿＿＿＿＿＿＿＿＿＿ ?

Structure　복합 부사구

The degree to which the Earth is cooled depends on many variables, such as the size and composition of the participles, as well as the reflective properties of the materials on the Earth's surface immediately below the aerosols.

○ The degree란 어떤 온도를 말하는가?
   → ＿＿＿＿＿＿＿＿＿＿＿＿＿ (해석)

○ many variables란 어떤 변수들을 말하는지 두 가지 쓰시오.
   → ＿＿＿＿＿＿＿＿＿＿＿＿＿
   → ＿＿＿＿＿＿＿＿＿＿＿＿＿

문장의 구조	주어 + 동사 + 목적어 + (부사구) + (부사구) + (부사구) + (부사구)

- 주어 → ＿＿＿＿＿＿＿＿＿＿
- 동사 → ＿＿＿＿＿＿＿＿＿＿
- 목적어 → ＿＿＿＿＿＿＿＿＿＿
- (부사구) → ＿＿＿＿＿＿＿＿＿＿

- (부사구) → ＿＿＿＿＿＿＿＿＿＿
- (부사구) → ＿＿＿＿＿＿＿＿＿＿
- (부사구) → ＿＿＿＿＿＿＿＿＿＿

Writing

다음 밑줄 친 우리말을 문맥에 맞게 영작하시오.

1. Aerosols ~하는 효과를 지니고 있다 cooling the Earth's surface.

    └→

2. The degree 여러 가지 변수에 따라 다르다, such as the size and composition of the particles, as well as the reflective properties.

    └→

3. The cooling effect of aerosols will counteract the greenhouse effect ~을 덥혀 오고 있는 the Earth's surface for the last few decades.

    └→

4. In fact, without aerosols in the atmosphere, 구름도 없을 것이다.

    └→

5. (~가 …하는 데에) 더 많은 시간이 걸리다 for small drops to coalesce into drops that are large enough to fall to the ground.

    └→

Before the "ignition button" is pushed to launch a satellite, an enormous number of obstacles have usually been overcome. Projects of this nature normally have tons of hiccups along the way and Terra, launched on December 18, 1999, was no exception to this rule. Terra Project Manager Kevin Grady is a positive manager who sees the glass as half full rather than half empty. And he needed to overcome the obstacles in the project's way.

The first obstacle was that Grady's veteran launch team had to master a new flight operation system that had never before been used by NASA. Six months before the initial launch date in December 1998, mission managers realized that the flight operation system that they had been working with had too many problems and they decided to abandon it and adopt a new one. Consequently, the launch date was delayed for six months.

Then close to the launch date a company supplying rockets that would be used to launch Terra into space discovered that the rocket's engine had a serious problem which could cause a launch failure. Since they had to fix or replace it with a new one, a new launch date had to be set, again!

As the new date of December 16 approached, Grady kept his team thinking positively, telling them "Spacecraft operations and activation provide opportunities for us to excel." On the 16th, Grady thought his team was "well prepared" and there would be no further delays. Even though Grady and his team were well prepared, Terra stood ready on the launch pad another 48 hours before lift off.

Words
_____

- ignition [igníʃən] 점화 · satellite [sǽtəlàit] 위성 · enormous [inɔ́ːrməs] 막대한, 거대한 · obstacle [ɑ́bstəkəl] 장애(물)
- hiccup [híkʌp] 딸꾹질, 약간의 문제 · exception [iksépʃən] 예외, 제외 · adopt [ədɑ́pt] 채택하다
- replace A with B A를 B로 교체하다 · activation [æ̀ktivéiʃən] 활성(화) · launch pad 발사대

Info Scan **1.** Which of the following is correct?

① The Terra Project Manager was not very experienced in launching satellites.
② It took 48 hours for the team to set the satellite Terra on the launch pad.
③ Launch team had to repair the previous operation system for almost a year.
④ The first launch attempt failed because of one of the rocket engines.
⑤ It took several months for the team to learn about the new operation system.

Reference **2.** 밑줄 친 it이 가리키는 말을 본문에서 찾아 쓰시오.

....

Analysis **3.** Terra Project의 두 가지 장애물로 언급된 것을 우리말로 설명하시오.

....

....

Detail **4.** How many times was the Terra launch postponed? (in English)

....

Grammar   대명사 one 과 it

- They decided to abandon it and adopt a new one.
- They had to fix or replace it with a new one.
+ Do you need a pen? — Yes, I need one. <a pen>
+ Do you need this pen? — Yes, I need it. <the pen>

Tips   one은 셀 수 있는 명사의 반복을 피하기 위해서 사용(즉, 대명사로 사용)하는데 '같은 종류'의 것을 나타낸다. 복수형은
ones이다. 한편, 비특정의 것을 가리키는 one과 달리, 특정한 것을 지칭할 때는 it이나 that을 사용한다.

Quiz   다음을 영작하시오.

1. 너는 노트북 컴퓨터가 있니? — 아니, 하지만 우리 오빠는 하나 있어. 그는 그것을 어제 샀거든.
   → Do you have a notebook computer?
   — No, but my brother _____ . He _____ yesterday.
2. 미국의 수도는 일본의 수도보다 더 크다.
   → The capital of the U.S.A. is larger _____ .

Structure   형용사절의 명사 수식

The flight operation system that they had been working with had too many problems.

   ◎ The flight operation system은 어떤 운영 시스템을 말하는가?

   → ....
   → (해석) ....

문장의 구조	주어 + 동사 + 목적어

- 주어 → ....
- 동사 → ....
- 목적어 → ....

다음 밑줄 친 우리말을 문맥에 맞게 영작하시오.

1. Terra, launched on December 18, 1999, 이 규칙에 예외가 아니었다.

   └,

2. Terra Project Manager Kevin Grady is a positive manager who sees the glass as half full 절반 비었다기보다는.

   └,

3. The first obstacle was that Grady's veteran launch team had to master a new flight operation system that 전혀 사용되어 본 적이 없었다 by NASA.

   └,

4. A company supplying rockets ~을 발사시키는 데 사용될 Terra into space discovered that the rocket's engine had a serious problem.

   └,

5. Grady thought his team was "well prepared" and 더 이상의 지연은 없을 것이다.

   └,

Review

A 다음 단어의 뜻을 쓰시오.

01. adopt _____
02. coalesce _____
03. eruption _____
04. fossil _____
05. hypothesize _____
06. inhabit _____

07. interfere with _____
08. minute *a.*_____
09. obstacle _____
10. preserve _____
11. satellite _____
12. sequence _____

B A의 단어를 활용하여 다음 우리말에 맞게 영작하시오.

01. 사소한 차이들 _____
02. 화산의 폭발 _____
03. 보존 식품 _____
04. 숲에 서식하다 _____
05. 성공에의 장애물 _____
06. 문화의 발전을 저해하다 _____

C A의 단어를 활용하여 다음 문장의 빈칸에 문맥상 알맞은 말을 쓰시오.

01. A(n) _____ is the remains or evidence of any creature that once lived on the Earth.

02. If two or more things _____, they come together and form a larger group or system.

03. If you _____ a new attitude, plan, or way of behaving, you begin to have it.

04. If you _____ that something will happen, you think that thing will happen because of various facts you have considered.

05. A(n) _____ is an object that goes around, or orbits, a larger object, such as a planet.

06. A(n) _____ of events or things is a number of events or things that come one after another in a particular order.

D   다음 문장의 빈칸에 어법상 알맞은 것을 고르시오.

01. We found the place very large and _____.

① not too crowded   ② too not crowded   ③ crowded not too

02. She can either ask for a bonus or _____.

① has a paid vacation   ② have a paid vacation   ③ can have a paid vacation

03. The shape and the color of your phone are much better than _____.

① mine   ② that of mine   ③ those of mine

04. He is not an actor but _____.

① sings a song   ② singing songs   ③ a singer

05. I don't have a pen. But I can borrow _____ from my friends.

① one   ② the one   ③ that

06. He _____ at work. (그는 항상 바쁜 것은 아니다.)

① is always not busy   ② is not always busy   ③ is not busy always

07. _____, I wouldn't have succeeded in the project.

① If it is not for you   ② Without your helping me   ③ Without you helped me

08. Would it be possible for me to earn that much money _____?

① but your assisting   ② but your assistance for   ③ but for your assistance

09. Losing _____ mean failure.

① necessarily does not   ② does necessarily not   ③ does not necessarily

10. _____ interesting. (모든 쇼가 재미있는 것은 아니다.)

① Not every show is   ② Every show is not   ③ All shows are not

Chapter 02

Vocabulary Pre-check

알고 있는 단어에 체크하고 단어들의 뜻을 쓰시오.

abruptly	gymnastics
adhere to	hygiene
alter	immense
aqueduct	impose
artificial	imprison
association	incredible
astronomer	ingredient
attain	intricate
be concerned about	mass produce
be familiar with	mimic
be released from	molecule
canal	no longer
civil engineer	nourishment
colossal	pass on to
consumption	pill
contrary to	predict
critical	preservation
curl	protein
curve	purity
despicable	reform
devotee	reincarnation
discard v.	release
distribution	reliable
diversity	removal
dose	resident
ensure	reveal
eruption	rigid
feasible	sect
feat	sewage
feed	sophisticated
flap	subject
flatten	suck
flexible	tablet
fountain	territory
genetically	tyrant
gradient	uncertainty

The bat world is full of diversity. Not only do different types of bats have different diets, ranging from fruits to insects, but also some bats use sound waves to move around while others use eyes. Moreover, of the over 1,200 species of bats in the world, only a few suck blood for nourishment. But what all bats have in common is, other than being the only flying mammals in existence, flexible wings that allow them to perform flying <u>feats</u>. Bats change direction very quickly, turning up, down or around abruptly and unexpectedly.

(A) High-speed video cameras have been used to film the flying motions of bats, revealing details about the mechanisms of bat flight. (B) The intricate nature of the bats' flight patterns shocked scientists at first because they were so much different than the flight patterns of birds which scientists thought would be similar to bats. (C) Bats never flatten their wings like an airplane when they are flying. Rather the wings of bats curve, curl, and change direction constantly as they fly. (D) Even if airplanes flapped their wings like bats, they still wouldn't be mimicking accurately the flight pattern of bats. (E)

Scientists will continue studying the flight patterns of bats in the hope that they can one day be able to design airplanes and other types of flying machines that will fly like bats do. Bat-like flying machines could be a big help fighting in war and in emergency situations like fires, earthquakes, or volcanic eruptions, to rescue people from tight, collapsed spaces or perform other tasks.

Words

• **diversity** [divə́ːrsəti] 다양성, 변화 • **suck** [sʌk] 빨다, 빨아 먹다 • **nourishment** [nə́ːriʃmənt] 음식물, 영양 • **mammal** [mǽməl] 포유류
• **flexible** [fléksəbəl] 유연한, 구부리기 쉬운 • **abruptly** [əbrʌ́ptli] 갑작스럽게 • **reveal** [rivíːl] 드러내다 • **intricate** [íntrəkit] 복잡한, 뒤얽힌
• **flatten** [flǽtn] 평평하게 하다 • **rather** [rǽðər] 오히려 • **curve** [kəːrv] 구부리다 • **curl** [kəːrl] 감다, 비틀다
• **flap** [flæp] (날개를) 펄럭이다 • **mimic** [mímik] 흉내내다, 모방하다 • **volcanic** [vɑlkǽnik] 화산의 • **eruption** [irʌ́pʃən] 분출

Info Scan **1.** According to the passage, which of the following is NOT true?

① Some bats rely on their eyes to see things.
② Some bats depend on sound waves to fly around.
③ Some bats eat vegetables while others drink animal blood.
④ Bats' flight patterns are very similar to those of many birds.
⑤ Scientists are trying to create a machine that can fly like a bat.

Analysis **2.** 새나 비행기와 다른 박쥐 비행의 특징을 우리말로 설명하시오.

Coherence **3.** (A)~(E) 중, 글의 흐름상 주어진 문장이 들어가기 가장 적절한 곳은?

> That is because the curving and curling of the wing is the key which allows bats to fly the way they do.

① (A)   ② (B)   ③ (C)
④ (D)   ⑤ (E)

Vocabulary **4.** 밑줄 친 feats와 바꾸어 쓸 수 있는 말은?

① patterns
② abilities
③ courses
④ stunts
⑤ directions

Grammar 삽입구문

- What all bats have in common is, (other than being the only flying mammals in existence,) flexible wings that allow them to perform flying feats.
- They were so much different than the flight patterns of birds which (scientists thought) would be similar to bats.

Tips 삽입이란 글 안에 보충 설명을 위해 다른 어구나 절을 첨가하는 경우를 말한다. 삽입의 시작과 끝을 명백하게 하기 위해, 앞뒤에 콤마(,)나 ―를 넣어주기도 한다. 삽입 형태의 말은 단지 꾸며 주는 역할만 하므로, 생략해도 남아 있는 문장이 문법적으로 완벽해야 한다.

Quiz 다음을 영작하시오.

1. 그는, 내가 믿기로는, 위대한 정치가이다. → He is, _____, a great statesman.

2. 그녀는, 내가 보기에는, 매우 활동적이고 창조적이다. (seem) → She is, _____, very active and creative.

3. 한번 내뱉은 말은, 일단 발사된 탄환처럼, 회수될 수 없다. (bullet, fire)
   → Words once spoken, _____, can't be recalled.

Structure what/if/whether가 이끄는 명사절

What all bats have in common is, other than being the only flying mammals in existence, flexible wings that allow them to perform flying feats.

◎ 이 문장에서 삽입된 전치사구는?
   → ....

◎ 주어 What의 보어가 되는 말은?
   → ....

문장의 구조	주어 + 동사 + (전치사구) + 보어 + (관계사절)

- 주어 → ....
- 동사 → ....
- (전치사구) → ....

- 보어 → ....
- (관계사절) → ....

Writing

다음 밑줄 친 우리말을 문맥에 맞게 영작하시오.

1. 다양한 종류의 박쥐들은 ~을 가지고 있을 뿐만 아니라 different diets, but also some bats use sound waves to move around.

    └,

2. 모든 박쥐들이 공통적으로 갖는 것은 is flexible wings that allow them to perform flying feats.

    └,

3. They were so much different than the flight patterns of birds which scientists thought 박쥐와 비슷할 것이다.

    └,

4. Bats 날개를 결코 평평하게 하지 않는다 like an airplane when they are flying.

    └,

5. That is because the curving and curling of the wing is the key which 박쥐로 하여금 그들이 하는 그런 방법으로 날 수 있게 하다.

    └,

Pythagoras is believed to have journeyed to Egypt, Babylon and then Samos so that he could study advanced mathematics. After a while, he and his devotees left Samos because of political uncertainties and the despicable actions of Samos's tyrant Polikrates. They established a kind of sect in southern Italy. Unlike many other sects of the day, they accepted women as their members who were highly respected in the region.

Since Pythagoras also believed in reincarnation, he was deeply concerned about the preservation of the soul and its purity. The sect wanted to end the process of reincarnation so that the soul could finally be released from the body which was believed to be imprisoning the soul. To achieve release, the sect focused on improving self-discipline by adhering to rigid rules about hygiene and eating. Also, the sect members studied the principal subjects, including mathematics, music, gymnastics and medicine for five years while keeping silent. It is unknown whether all these rules were imposed by Pythagoras himself or were the products of his followers.

In addition, contrary to popular belief, it was not Pythagoras who discovered the famous "sentence of Pythagoras" but the Babylonians. Babylonian astronomers had discovered that the orbits of the bodies in the sky followed mathematical patterns and _____. Pythagoras is also known to have influenced reforms in the political system since the "associations" started by his followers often managed to attain immense political influence in a given territory.

Words _____

• **devotee** [dèvoutíː] 열성가 • **tyrant** [táiərənt] 폭군 • **sect** [sekt] 학파 • **reincarnation** [rìːinkɑːrnéiʃən] 환생
• **preservation** [prèzərvéiʃən] 보호, 보존 • **purity** [pjúərəti] 순수, 청결 • **imprison** [impríz∂n] 가두다 • **release** [rilíːs] 해방(하다)
• **adhere to** ~을 고수하다 • **rigid** [rídʒid] 엄격한 • **hygiene** [háidʒiːn] 위생 상태, 청결함 • **gymnastics** [dʒimnǽstiks] 체육
• **impose** [impóuz] 부과하다 • **astronomer** [əstrɑ́nəmər] 천문학자 • **reform** [riːfɔ́ːrm] 개혁 • **immense** [iméns] 막대한
• **territory** [térətɔ̀ːri] 영토

1. According to the passage, which of the following is NOT correct?

① Pythagoras had much political influence on the society.
② Pythagoras and his followers were highly admired.
③ Pythagoras made strict rules of self-discipline and study.
④ Pythagoras believed that his spirit would be born again.
⑤ Pythagoras allowed even females in his sect as members.

2. 밑줄 친 despicable과 바꾸어 쓸 수 있는 단어가 아닌 것은?

① brutal
② vicious
③ cruel
④ savage
⑤ considerate

3. 빈칸에 들어갈 가장 적절한 말은?

① could be released
② could be predicted
③ could be varied
④ could be controlled
⑤ could be rearranged

4. What are the rules imposed by the sect of Pythagoras? (in Korean)

 ## Grammar 부정사의 완료시제

- Pythagoras is believed to have journeyed to Egypt, Babylon and then Samos.
- Pythagoras is also known to have influenced reforms in the political system.

Tips 부정사가 나타내는 시제에는 2가지가 있다. 하나는 단순부정사이고 또 하나는 완료부정사이다. 부정사의 완료시제는 부정사가 들어 있는 문장의 시제보다 그 이전의 시제를 나타낸다. 즉, 주문장의 시제가 현재이면 완료부정사는 과거를 나타내고, 주문장의 시제가 과거이면 완료부정사는 과거 이전의 일 즉, 대과거를 나타낸다.

| Quiz 완료부정사를 이용하여 다음을 영작하시오.

1. 그는 젊었을 때 부유했던 것 같다.
   → He _____ in his youth.
2. Michael Jordan은 최고의 농구선수였다고 믿어진다.
   → Michael Jordan is _____ the best basketball player.

 ## Structure 분사구의 명사 수식

The "associations" started by his followers often managed to attain immense political influence in a given territory.

◎ associations란 어떤 단체를 말하는가?

→ ....

→ (해석) ....

문장의 구조	주어 + 동사 + 목적어 + (전치사구)

- 주어 → .... • 목적어 → ....
- 동사 → .... • (전치사구) → ....

* 동사 manage가 뒤에 부정사를 목적어를 취하는 것으로 취급하였다.

Writing

다음 밑줄 친 우리말을 문맥에 맞게 영작하시오.

1. Unlike many other sects of the day, they accepted women as their members 그 지역에서 대단히 존경받는.

    └→ ....

2. Pythagoras also 환생을 믿었다.

    └→ ....

3. The soul could finally ~에서 벗어나지다 the body.

    └→ ....

4. The sect focused on improving self-discipline 엄격한 규칙을 고수함으로써 about hygiene and eating.

    └→ ....

5. ~인지 아닌지 알려져 있지 않다 all these rules were imposed by Pythagoras himself or were the products of his followers.

    └→ ....

The ancient Romans were excellent civil engineers, constructing colossal buildings which were incredible engineering achievements of their time. While most people are quite familiar with the Colosseum and other Roman architectural achievements, few know about the Roman system of aqueducts.

Aqueducts that carried water into Roman cities allowed Roman citizens living within large cities to enjoy fresh, clear water in a variety of ways. Not only is the supply of fresh water critical to the life of any resident of a large city, but the removal of dirty water is also important. So the Romans built this sophisticated water distribution system to take away dirty, sewage-filled water as well.

The aqueducts the Romans built were really a system of canals. Water originated from a spot from which it flowed naturally, a spring for example. Then they constructed aqueducts to transport the water into the cities. Canals couldn't be built within cities so the Romans used a series of tanks and pipes to ensure that every area within a given city was able to receive fresh water and discard dirty water. The engineering marvel of the whole system was ensuring that the system of canals and pipes had a constant gradient so that clean water flowed in and dirty water flowed out at a steady speed without any assistance.

With such a reliable supply of water within the heart of its cities, the Romans built fountains, public baths and artificial lakes. In Rome alone there were 1,200 fountains, 11 public baths and 2 artificial lakes.

Words

- civil engineer 토목 기사   - colossal [kəlásəl] 거대한, 광장한   - incredible [inkrédəbəl] 믿을 수 없는
- be familiar with ~을 잘 알고 있다   - aqueduct [ǽkwədʌ̀kt] 수로, 도수관   - critical [krítikəl] 꼭 필요한
- resident [rézidənt] 거주자   - removal [rimú:vəl] 제거   - distribution [dìstrəbjú:ʃən] 보급, 배분   - sewage [sú:idʒ] 하수 오물
- as well 게다가, ~도 또한   - canal [kənǽl] 운하   - spot [spɑt] 장소, 지점   - discard [diskɑ́:rd] 버리다
- gradient [gréidiənt] 경사도, 기울기

Info Scan

1. Which of the following is correct according to the passage? (choose two)

① The Roman aqueduct was invented and developed during several wars.

② Water was supplied from water sources in cities to each home.

③ Ample water supplies allowed Roman people to build various facilities.

④ The aqueducts could be adjusted to control of the amount of waterflow.

⑤ The system used a steady slope for the right speed of water flow.

Analysis

2. aqueduct의 두 가지 주요 기능을 우리말로 쓰시오.

....

....

Detail

3. 로마의 aqueduct를 뜻하는 다른 표현을 본문에서 모두 찾아 쓰시오.

....

....

....

Vocabulary

4. 밑줄 친 sophisticated와 바꾸어 쓸 수 있는 말은?

① cost efficient   ② very simple

③ man-made   ④ complex

⑤ natural

 ## Grammar   so that 구문

- The system of canals and pipes had a constant gradient so that clean water flowed in and dirty water flowed out.

+ She worked hard so that she could succeed.
  = She worked hard (in order (so as)) to succeed.
  = She worked hard in order that she could succeed.

> Tips so that은 '~하기 위해서'라는 목적을 나타낸다. 〈in order (for + 목적어) to부정사〉 또는 〈so as (for + 목적어) to부정사〉로 바꾸어 쓸 수 있다.

┃ Quiz 다음을 so that 구문을 이용하여 영작하시오.

1. 우리는 말하는 것보다 두 배만큼 들을 수 있기 위해서, 두 개의 귀와 하나의 입을 가지고 있다.
   → We have two ears and one mouth _____ as much as we speak.

2. We will do our best in order for them to look forward to a bright future.
   → We will do our best _____ a bright future.

 ## Structure   형용사절의 명사 수식

Aqueducts that carried water into Roman cities allowed Roman citizens living within large cities to enjoy fresh, clear water in a variety of ways.

⊙ Aqueducts란 어떤 수로를 말하는가?
   → ....
   → (해석)

⊙ Roman citizens이란 어떤 사람들을 말하는가?
   → ....

문장의 구조	주어 + 동사 + 목적어 + 목적격보어 + (전치사구)

- 주어 → ....
- 동사 → ....
- 목적어 → ....

- 목적격보어 → ....
- (전치사구) → ....

다음 밑줄 친 우리말을 문맥에 맞게 영작하시오.

Writing

1. While most people ~을 상당히 잘 알고 있다 the Colosseum, few know about the Roman system of aqueducts.

   └

2. ~의 공급이 …할 뿐만 아니라 of fresh water critical to the life of any resident of a large city, but the removal of dirty water is also important.

   └

3. The Romans built this sophisticated water distribution system 오물로 가득한 물을 버리기 위해서도.

   └

4. Water originated from a spot ~로부터 자연적으로 물이 흘렀던, a spring for example.

   └

5. The system 일정한 기울기를 갖고 있었다 so that clean water flowed in and dirty water flowed out at a steady speed without any assistance.

   └

Medicine can come in the form of capsules, tablets or powder which we take with water. It can also come in the form of cream which we apply to our skin. Now scientists are trying to genetically engineer medicines into our food. No longer would you have to take your pills after eating your eggs for breakfast as the eggs would have the medicine already in them.

This is possible because drugs are made of protein molecules. Animals make thousands of proteins, the main ingredient in skin, hair, milk, and meat. If drugs are made from the proteins, then animals can be genetically engineered to produce the drugs themselves.

In fact, sheep, cows and goats have already been genetically engineered by scientists to produce protein drugs which are collected in those animals' milk. Chickens, however, are the best choice to mass produce drugs for human consumption since they grow fastest. Chickens are also cheap to feed and easy to take care of. Since chickens don't produce milk, people would simply eat some eggs to get their needed daily dose of medicine. The scientists altered the chickens' DNA so that the birds make these drugs only in their egg whites. This protects the chickens' bodies from the drugs' possible harmful effects and makes it easy for scientists to collect the drugs.

Researchers in this field have already produced two types of chickens whose eggs contain protein drugs. One produces a drug to treat skin cancer and the other produces a drug to treat multiple sclerosis, a nerve disorder. These researchers have discovered that the chickens pass on to their chicks their drug creating abilities, making the whole project much more economically feasible. Nevertheless, more testing still needs to be done before these 'medicine eggs' reach your local grocery store.

Words

• **tablet** [tǽblit] 정제　• **apply to** ~에 바르다　• **genetically** [dʒinétikəli] 유전학적으로　• **protein** [próutiːin] 단백질
• **molecule** [mɑ́ləkjùːl] 분자　• **ingredient** [ingríːdiənt] 성분, 재료　• **take care of** ~을 돌보다　• **dose** [dous] (약의) 1회분
• **egg white** 계란의 흰자위　• **multiple sclerosis** 다발성경화증　• **pass on to** ~에게 물려주다　• **feasible** [fíːzəbəl] 편리한, 용이한

Info Scan
1. According to the passage which of the following is NOT true?

① Several animals including chickens are used to produce medicine.

② Animals with genetically altered DNA can produce drugs themselves.

③ Drugs are made of proteins that are the main elements of many body parts.

④ Harmful side effects have not been found in animal drugs in the market.

⑤ Some animals have been successfully engineered to produce various medicines.

Analysis
2. Explain why chickens are favored as an animal for mass production. (in Korean)

....

....

....

Analysis
3. 과학자들이 흰자위에만 약을 만들도록 조정한 이유 두 가지를 우리말로 설명하시오.

....

....

Inference
4. Which of the following can be inferred from the passage?

① The ability to make drugs can't be passed on to another generation.

② Most diseases can be treated by protein drugs in the near future.

③ A few types of these eggs are now available in some local markets.

④ Changing the DNA of every chicken to make drugs is not necessary.

⑤ It will take years to produce enough eggs for human consumption.

Grammar   가목적어 it

- This makes it easy *for scientists to collect the drugs*.
- [+] I think it useless *to find fault with her*.

Tips to부정사구가 목적어로 쓰일 때 글의 균형을 잡기 위해서 to부정사구 대신 it을 쓰고 to부정사구를 뒤로 보내는 경우가 있다. 이 때 사용된 it을 가목적어(형식목적어)라고 하고 뒤로 보내진 to부정사구를 진목적어라고 한다. 한편, to부정사의 의미상의 주어는 〈for+목적격〉으로 나타낼 수 있다.

▍ Quiz 다음을 영작하시오.

1. 나는 매일 일기를 쓰는 것을 규칙으로 하고 있다. → I make _____ keep a diary every day.

2. 그녀는 그 문제에 대해서 아무 말도 하지 않는 것이 최선이라고 여겼다. (say nothing)
   → She considered _____ about the matter.

3. 어떤 톨게이트에서는 컴퓨터가 차량들이 톨게이트를 통과하는 것을 수월하게 해 준다. (pass)
   → Computers in some tollgates make _____ through them.

Structure   to부정사의 다양한 용법

Sheep, cows and goats have already been genetically engineered by scientists to produce protein drugs which are collected in those animals' milk.

  ◉ to produce는 부정사의 어떤 용법인가?

   → _____ (해석)

  ◉ protein drugs는 어떤 약을 말하는가?

   → _____ (해석)

문장의 구조	주어 + 동사 + 보어 + (+전치사구) + (부정사구) + (관계대명사절)

- 주어   → ....
- 동사   → ....
- 보어   → ....

- (전치사구)   → ....
- (부정사구)   → ....
- (관계대명사절) → ....

Writing

다음 밑줄 친 우리말을 문맥에 맞게 영작하시오.

1. It can also come in the form of cream 우리가 피부에 바를 수 있는.

   └﹁

2. 더 이상 ~할 필요가 없을 것이다 take your pills after eating your eggs for breakfast.

   └﹁

3. Chickens are also cheap to feed and 돌보기 쉬운.

   └﹁

4. The chickens pass on to their chicks their drug creating abilities, making the whole project 훨씬 더 경제적으로 수월하게.

   └﹁

5. Nevertheless, 여전히 더 많은 실험이 행해져야 할 필요가 있다 before these 'medicine eggs' reach your local grocery store.

   └﹁

Review

A 다음 단어의 뜻을 쓰시오.

01. adhere to _____

02. artificial _____

03. despicable _____

04. devotee _____

05. distribution _____

06. feat _____

07. gradient _____

08. hygiene _____

09. mammal _____

10. mimic _____

11. reincarnation _____

12. reliable _____

B A의 단어를 활용하여 다음 우리말에 맞게 영작하시오.

01. 믿을 수 있는 친구 _____

02. 믿을 수 없는 묘기 _____

03. 인공의 꽃, 조화 _____

04. 부의 분배 (wealth) _____

05. 환생을 믿다 _____

06. 고래는 포유동물이다. (Whales) _____

C A의 단어를 활용하여 다음 문장의 빈칸에 문맥상 알맞은 말을 쓰시오.

01. To _____ to something is to stick to it.

02. A(n) _____ is a slope, or the degree to which the ground slopes.

03. Someone who is a(n) _____ of a subject or activity is very enthusiastic about it.

04. Oral _____ is the practice of keeping the mouth and teeth clean in order to prevent dental problems and bad breath.

05. If you say that people or actions are _____, you are emphasizing that they are extremely nasty, cruel, or evil.

06. If you _____ the actions or voice of people or animals, you imitate them, usually in a way that is meant to be amusing or entertaining.

D 다음 문장의 빈칸에 어법상 알맞은 것을 고르시오.

01. I bought my own car _____ leave anytime.
　　① so that I could　　　　② that I could　　　　③ in order to I could

02. The artist is believed _____ many paintings.
　　① to be left　　　　② to have left　　　　③ to have been left

03. They considered _____ all the food in the refrigerator.
　　① useless it to bring　　② it useless to bring　　③ it is useless bring

04. _____ didn't enjoy the play. (John은, 다른 아이들처럼,)
　　① John likely with other kids　　② John like other kids　　③ John, like other kids,

05. We left our name cards _____ contact us later.
　　① in order to their　　　② that they could　　　③ so that they could

06. Don't make _____ find it later.
　　① it for me hard to　　　② it is hard to　　　③ it hard for me to

07. The professor is known _____ in France.
　　① to be studied　　　② to have been studied　　③ to have studied

08. _____ very smart and humorous. (그는, 내가 보기에는,)
　　① He is, it seems to me,　　② I seem he is　　　③ He seems me he is

09. I think _____ drive your car.
　　① it is fine let him　　　② it fine to let him　　　③ it fine he

10. She seems to _____ a lot when she lived abroad.
　　① go through　　　② gone through　　　③ have gone through

Chapter 03

Vocabulary Pre-check

알고 있는 단어에 체크하고 단어들의 뜻을 쓰시오.

alertness	inherit
astronomer	insight
authorial	intermingle
be cloaked in	intriguing
blistering	invisible
cue	locale
compelling	magnet
complication	maintain
component	Mercury
composition	microscope
confusion	narrative
cram	nod off
current *a.*	oversized
define	paradox
deflect	participant
distinct	perplexed
dominate	Pluto
drift	protagonist
edge	radiation
emit	reveal
extremely	seemingly
flashback	shepherd
gadget	subject
giant *a.*	telescope
gravity	tension
haze	thematically
imprecise	tissue
in response to	unfold
infrared	vacuum

A synchrotron is a machine which is as long and wide as a football field. It might be mistaken for an inventor's oversized gadget, but it is not a gadget. It is a powerful machine that uses tubes, magnets, vacuum pumps, and other gadgetry to produce intensely powerful beams of light. (A) Scientists are using this huge machine to look deeper than ever into the structure of atoms and cells. (B) Everyone knows about microscopes that let you see what the eye can't see, and this is like the next level of microscope.

(C) A synchrotron uses giant magnets, radio waves, and something called an electron gun to push electrons until they move at a blistering 99.9987 percent of the speed of light. (D) Electrons moving that quickly produce extremely bright light. Magnets direct this light into beams, known as beamlines. (E) Each beamline can be designed to emit just one type of light, ranging from infrared to X rays, with a very specific amount of energy.

The synchrotron can be used to treat diseases. For example, doctors often use X rays to kill cancer cells. Radiation treatments are imprecise, however, and many healthy cells die in the process. By using the highly focused synchrotron X-ray beam, scientists hope to destroy individual cancer cells without harming healthy tissue.

Not only can this technology be used by medical companies, but the technology can also be used by food companies for better tasting foods. The synchrotron's X-ray beam was used by a chocolate manufacturer to discover the ideal temperature for processing chocolate.

Words _____

• **oversized** [óuvərsáizd] 너무 큰, 특대의 • **gadget** [gǽdʒit] (간단한) 장치 • **magnet** [mǽgnit] 자석 • **vacuum** [vǽkjuəm] 진공
• **microscope** [máikrouskòup] 현미경 • **blistering** [blístəriŋ] 굉장한 • **infrared** [ìnfrəréd] 적외선의
• **radiation** [rèidiéiʃən] 방사성(의) • **imprecise** [ìmprəsáis] 부정확한 • **tissue** [tíʃuː] 조직 • **insight** [ínsàit] 통찰력

Info Scan

1. According to the passage, which of the following is NOT true about the synchrotron?

① It was invented to produce intensely powerful beams of light.
② It makes electrons move incredibly close to the speed of light.
③ It can give off one specific type of light for a specific purpose.
④ It can control the amount of energy depending on the purpose.
⑤ It produces magnetic energy which turns into bright beamlines.

Analysis

2. 암을 치료함에 있어 X ray와 싱크로트론 X ray의 차이점을 설명하시오.

• 기존의 X ray:

• 싱크로트론 X ray:

Inference

3. Why does the author mention microscopes?

① to give a brief idea of the shape of the synchrotron and its parts
② to imply that the synchrotron will replace microscopes at present
③ to show how objects are observed with the synchrotron machine
④ to help the understanding of the overall purpose of the synchrotron
⑤ to explain the synchrotron should be much smaller than it is now

Coherence

4. (A)~(E) 중, 글의 흐름상 주어진 문장이 들어가기 가장 적절한 곳은?

The work is giving them insights into the human body and the world.

① (A)   ② (B)   ③ (C)
④ (D)   ⑤ (E)

Grammar   to부정사의 부사적 용법

- It is a powerful machine that uses things to produce intensely powerful beams of light.
- Scientists are using this huge machine to look deeper than ever into the structure atoms and cells.
- The synchrotron can be used to treat diseases.

Tips 부정사가 부사처럼 동사, 형용사, 부사를 수식하는 경우 부사적 용법이라고 한다. 부사적 용법에서는 내용에 따라 '목적, 원인, 결과, 정도' 등의 뜻을 나타낸다.

❘ Quiz   다음을 to부정사를 사용하여 영작하시오.

1. 우리는 먹기 위해 사는 것이 아니라 살기 위해서 먹는다. → We do not live to eat, but _____.

2. 어느 날 아침, 잠에서 깨어 유명해져 있는 나 자신을 발견했다. → One morning I _____.

Structure   to부정사의 다양한 용법

A synchrotron uses giant magnets, radio waves, and something called an electron gun to push electrons until they move at a blistering 99.9987 percent of the speed of light.

◎ A synchrotron이 사용하는 것을 모두 쓰시오.

→ _____

→ _____

→ _____

문장의 구조	주어 + 동사 + 목적어 + (부사적 부정사구)		

- 주어 → _____
- 목적어 → _____
- 동사 → _____
- (부정사구) → _____

Writing

다음 밑줄 친 우리말을 문맥에 맞게 영작하시오.

1. A synchrotron is a machine which is ~만큼 길고 넓은 a football field.

   └,

2. Scientists are using this huge machine 그 어느 때보다 더 깊이 보기 위해 into the structure of atoms and cells.

   └,

3. Everyone knows about microscopes that 눈으로 볼 수 없는 것을 당신이 보게 하다.

   └,

4. Each beamline can be designed to emit just one type of light, 적외선에서 엑스선에 이르기까지, with a very specific amount of energy.

   └,

5. 이 기술은 사용될 수 있을 뿐만 아니라 by medical companies, but the technology can also be used by food companies for better tasting foods.

   └,

Bill was up all night cramming for a biology test at school. Sue was too. Sue, however, didn't nod off during the test while Bill did. While this might seem like a paradox, researchers have known for a long time that different people have different sleep requirements. What has always perplexed researchers is why people have these different requirements. What they are now discovering is that our need for sleep has a genetic component. So Bill who received the F can only blame his parents for falling asleep during a test, while Sue has to go home and thank hers.

Researchers have recently discovered that one gene, the "clock gene," affects how well a person functions without sleep. It is a type of gene called a Period 3 gene. The Period 3 gene comes in two forms: short and long. Everyone has two copies of the gene. So you may have two longs, two shorts, or one of each. (A) The forms a person has depend on what he or she inherited from his or her parents.

(B) In a recent study, scientists studied test subjects who had stayed awake for 40 hours straight. (C) Then, these participants did a variety of tests to measure their mental alertness. (D) The results revealed that people who have short forms of this gene do much better with less or no sleep than people who have the long forms of the gene. (E) The researchers concluded that people with the long form of the Period 3 gene dealing with sleep simply needed more sleep to keep their brains working well.

Words _____

- cram [kræm] 주입시키다, 벼락공부를 하다 · biology [baiálədʒi] 생물학 · nod off 꾸벅꾸벅 졸다
- paradox [pǽrədàks] 역설, 앞뒤가 맞지 않는 · perplexed [pərplékst] 당혹한, 혼란스러운 · component [kəmpóunənt] 성분, 요소
- function [fʌ́ŋkʃən] 작용하다, 움직이다 · inherit [inhérit] 물려받다 · subject [sʌ́bdʒikt] 피실험자, 실험 대상자
- participant [pɑːrtísəpənt] 참가자, 참여자 · alertness [ələ́ːrtnis] 각성도 · in response to ~에 반응하여 · cue [ku:] 단서, 자극

Info Scan
1. According to the passage, which of the following is correct?

① Every person has at least one long form of the Period 3 gene.

② The combination of the Period 3 gene is variable while growing up.

③ A person might have one long and one short Period 3 gene.

④ There are many types of clock genes including the Period 3 gene.

⑤ The Period 3 gene basically gets longer as a person gets older.

Summary
2. 다음 빈칸에 알맞은 말을 넣어 실험 결과를 설명하시오.

➜ A person with short forms of the Period 3 gene needs
.............................., while a person with .... requires
.... to have their brains work at top form.

Coherence
3. (A)~(E) 중, 글의 흐름상 주어진 문장이 들어가기 가장 적절한 곳은?

For example, researchers tested how quickly they pushed
a button in response to a visual cue.

① (A)   ② (B)   ③ (C)
④ (D)   ⑤ (E)

Vocabulary
4. 다음 중 밑줄 친 perplexed의 의미와 가장 가까운 것은?

① surprised   ② puzzled   ③ burdened
④ bored   ⑤ helped

Grammar 비교급

- *People who have short forms of this gene* do much better with less or no sleep than *people who have the long forms of the gene.*

Tips 비교구문에서 비교의 대상이 되는 내용들끼리는 동일 범주의 문법 구조 및 동일 범주의 내용을 병치해야 한다. 한편, 비교급을 강조하는 부사적 표현에는 much, far, still, even, a lot 등이 있다.

| Quiz 다음을 영작하시오.

1. 이 꽃들은 저 꽃들보다 덜 예쁘지는 않다.
   → These flowers are not _____ those flowers.

2. 말의 타격은 칼의 타격보다 훨씬 더 심한 충격을 준다. (even, deep)
   → A blow with a word strikes _____ .

Structure what/if/whether가 이끄는 명사절

What has always perplexed researchers is why people have these different requirements.

◯ What과 동격인 것을 쓰시오.
   → (동격)

◯ 동격을 주어에 대입하여 문장을 다시 쓰시오.
   →

문장의 구조	주어 + 동사 + 보어

- 주어 →
- 동사 →
- 보어 →

Writing

다음 밑줄 친 우리말을 문맥에 맞게 영작하시오.

1. Bill 밤새 벼락치기 공부를 하느라 깨어 있었다 for a biology test at school.

   └→ ....

2. 이제 그들이 발견하고 있는 것은 is that our need for sleep has a genetic component.

   └, ...

3. Researchers have recently discovered that one gene, the "clock gene," affects 사람이 얼마나 잘 움직이는지[작동하는지] without sleep.

   └→ ....

4. 사람이 가지는 형태들은 depend on what he or she inherited from his or her parents.

   └→ ....

5. In a recent study, scientists studied test subjects 40시간 동안 줄곧 깨어 있었던.

   └→ ....

Novelists use many complex narrative structures to build tension and make stories more interesting for readers. And there are several authorial methods of achieving this.

One narrative structure or writing technique involves telling two or three different, seemingly unrelated stories, at the same time. Each story has different characters and is set in a different location. As a result, the jumping back and forth amongst the settings and characters can cause confusion for readers. Therefore time and place are usually clearly defined: events often occur within a very specific time frame in a specific locale to keep the reader focused. While the characters and locales in each story are not intermingled, the stories must be connected thematically.

Another complex narrative structure is the story within a story in which one central character is involved in several stories at the same time. While the central characters and the setting are the same in each story, different events are unfolding in each story. The stories are tied together not only by a protagonist but by thematic unity. Don Quixote is thought to be the first novel which employed this technique.

Novelists also alter the traditional time frame in order to make stories more interesting. The time frame can be altered by adding flashbacks. Or, as it was done by Emily Bronte in *Wuthering Heights*, the whole story can move backward and then forward, again and again, unfolding a compelling and intriguing drama. By using the complex narrative structure, Bronte was able to show how the past and the present are intermingled, and was able to maintain the theme of the story while adding interest by adding complication.

Words

- authorial [ɔːθɔ́ːriəl] 작가적인, 작가의 • seemingly [síːmiŋli] 보기에는 • define [difáin] 한정하다, 경계를 정하다
- locale [loukǽl] 장소, 현장 • intermingle [intərmíŋɡəl] 혼합하다, 섞다 • thematically [θimǽtickəli] 주제상으로
- unfold [ʌnfóuld] 펼치다, 벌리다 • flashback [flǽʃbæ̀k] 플래시백(과거 회상 장면으로의 전환)
- compelling [kəmpéliŋ] 강력한, 하지 않을 수 없는 • intriguing [intríːɡiŋ] 흥미를 자아내는 • complication [kàmpləkéiʃən] 복잡함

Info Scan **1.** According to paragraph 2, which of the following is true?

① Each story has to be unfolded one after another.

② Each story should not have many different settings.

③ Characters are often intermingled in different stories.

④ The settings of different stories are the same.

⑤ Different stories will include very similar events.

Analysis **2.** 이 글에 소개된 complex narrative를 만드는 세 가지 방법을 우리말로 설명하시오.

Analysis **3.** 이 글에 소개된 3가지 방법의 공통점을 우리말로 쓰시오.

Vocabulary **4.** 밑줄 친 protagonist와 바꾸어 쓸 수 있는 말은?

① reader of the story

② story itself

③ story author

④ leading character

⑤ cast of the story

Grammar 5형식 문장

- Novelists make *stories* more interesting for readers. ⋯▸ 형용사
- Events often occur within a specific time and locale to keep *the reader* focused. ⋯▸ 형용사
- ⁺Mr. Smith called *his son* a doctor. ⋯▸ 명사
- ⁺I got *him* to mend my watch. ⋯▸ 부정사

Tips 5형식 문장은 목적어 다음에 목적격보어가 오는 문장이다. 목적어와 목적격보어는 동격의 관계가 성립한다. 이 때 목적격 보어로는 명사, 형용사, 부정사 등이 올 수 있다.

┃ Quiz 다음을 영작하시오.

1. 인터넷은 세계를 하나의 세계적 사회로 만들고 있다. (global society)
   → The Internet is _____ .
2. 나는 나의 소망이 여러분들 안에서 자라나기를 바란다. (hope, grow)
   → I want _____ in you.

Structure 병렬

One narrative structure or writing technique involves telling two or three different, seemingly unrelated stories, at the same time.

◎ stories를 수식하는 말들을 모두 쓰시오.

→ ....

→ ....

→ (해석) ....

문장의 구조	주어 + 동사 + 목적어 + (전치사구)

- 주어 → ....
- 동사 → ....
- 목적어 → ....
- (전치사구) → ....

Writing

다음 밑줄 친 우리말을 문맥에 맞게 영작하시오.

1. Each story 다른 등장인물들을 가지고 있다 and is set in a different location.

    └→

    ....

2. While the characters and locales in each story are not intermingled, the stories 주제상으로는 연결되어 있어야 한다.

    └→

    ....

3. The stories are tied together 주인공에 의해서뿐만 아니라 but by thematic unity.

    └→

    ....

4. The time frame ~함으로써 바뀔 수 있다 adding flashbacks.

    └→

    ....

5. Bronte was able to show 과거와 현재가 어떻게 섞여 있는지.

    └→

    ....

Galileo Galilei, who was the first to use a telescope, wondered why Saturn sometimes looked different. Astronomers have now proven that the answer lies in the angle at which we view the plane of rings. At certain angles the rings are invisible, while at other angles they are clearly visible.

Astronomers are fascinated not only by Saturn's rings, but also by the 34 known moons, especially Titan, the largest moon orbiting Saturn. Bigger than Mercury and Pluto, Titan is intriguing because it is cloaked in a thick, smog-like haze and has its own atmosphere. Scientists believe that the atmosphere of early Earth was similar in composition to the current atmosphere on Titan. The climate, including wind and rain, creates surface features that are similar to those on Earth and like Earth, is dominated by seasonal weather patterns.

There are several small moons orbiting Saturn as well. A few, such as Pan, Atlas, Prometheus, and Pandora, which orbit near the outer edges of the rings or within gaps in the rings are known as "shepherd moons." The gravity of shepherd moons serves to maintain a sharply defined edge to the rings; material that drifts closer to the shepherd moons' orbits is either deflected back into the body of the rings or pulled into the moons themselves.

One moon, Enceladus, is one of the shiniest objects in the solar system. It's covered with white ice that reflects sunlight like freshly fallen snow. It's about as wide as Arizona. Another interesting moon orbiting Saturn is called Iapetus which has two distinct halves. One is as black as asphalt and the other is as bright as snow. All of Saturn's moons are unique and intriguing science targets.

Words

- telescope [téləskòup] 망원경 • angle [ǽŋgl] 각도 • plane [plein] (수)평면 • astronomer [əstránəmər] 천문학자
- moon [muːn] 위성 • Mercury [mə́ːrkjəri] 수성 • Pluto [pluːtou] 명왕성 • intriguing [intríːgiŋ] 호기심을 자아내는
- be cloaked in ~으로 덮여 있다 • haze [heiz] 안개, 아지랑이 • dominate [dámənèit] 우세하다, 특색지우다 • edge [edʒ] 가장자리, 테두리
- shepherd [ʃépərd] 양치기 • gravity [grǽvəti] 중력 • drift [drift] 떠돌다 • deflect [diflékt] 비끼게 하다, 빗나가게 하다

Info Scan

1. Which of the following is NOT correct? (choose two)

① Titan is the only moon in the solar system that is bigger than Mercury.

② Titan has a dense atmosphere and it is covered with a thick fog like haze.

③ Titan's atmosphere is very similar to Earth's before the beginning of life.

④ There are many small shepherd moons that are orbiting the moon Titan.

⑤ It was found that the weather of Titan is similar to that of the Earth.

Analysis

2. Galileo Galilei에게 Saturn이 때때로 다르게 보였던 이유를 우리말로 설명하시오.

....

Analysis

3. How do shepherd moons sharpen the edges of the rings? (in Korean)

....

Detail

4. Which of the following is mentioned as a reason for Enceladus to shine?

① half of the surface that is as bright as the sun

② freshly fallen snow that reflects most sunlight

③ the surface that is as wide as a state in the U.S.

④ the surface with white ice that reflects sunlight

⑤ the surface that is covered with clean snow

Grammar 동등비교

- It's about as wide as Arizona.
- One is as black as asphalt and the other is as bright as snow.
+ The moon is not so (as) large as the Earth.

Tips 둘 사이를 비교해서 같은 정도를 나타내는 비교의 형식을 '동등비교'라 하고 원급을 이용해서 나타낸다. 동등비교의 형식은 ⟨as+형용사+as⟩, 부정은 ⟨not as (so)+형용사+as⟩이다.

▌Quiz 다음을 동등비교를 이용하여 영작하시오.

1. 공기는 수질만큼 심하게 오염되었다. (badly)
   → The air is _____ the water.

2. 어떤 문제에 대한 답을 아는 것은 그 문제를 이해하는 것만큼 중요하지 않다.
   → Knowing the answer to a question _____ understanding the question.

Structure 전치사구의 수식을 받는 (동)명사구

A few, such as Pan, Atlas, Prometheus, and Pandora, which orbit near the outer edges of the rings or within gaps in the rings are known as "shepherd moons."

◎ a few의 예로 언급된 것은?
   → ....

◎ a few란 어떤 위성들을 말하는가?
   → ....
   → (해석)

문장의 구조	주어 + 동사 + 보어 + (전치사구)

- 주어 → ....
- 동사 → ....
- 보어 → ....
- (전치사구) → ....

Writing

다음 밑줄 친 우리말을 문맥에 맞게 영작하시오.

1. Galileo Galilei, who was the first to use a telescope, wondered 토성이
    왜 가끔 다르게 보였는지.

    └→

2. 어떤 각도에서는 고리가 보이지 않는다, while at other angles they are clearly
    visible.

    └→

3. Scientists believe that the atmosphere of early Earth 구성에 있어서 비슷
    했다 to the current atmosphere on Titan.

    └→

4. The climate creates surface features that are 지구의 그것들(특징들)과
    비슷한.

    └→

5. One is as black as asphalt and 다른 한 쪽은 눈처럼 환하다.

    └→

Review

A 다음 단어의 뜻을 쓰시오.

01. angle _____

02. cram _____

03. distinct _____

04. dominate _____

05. imprecise _____

06. inherit _____

07. intriguing _____

08. microscope _____

09. Pluto _____

10. protagonist _____

11. telescope _____

12. unfold _____

B A의 단어를 활용하여 다음 우리말에 맞게 영작하시오.

01. 어떤 각도에서(는) _____

02. 신문을 펼치다 _____

03. 부정확한 정보 _____

04. 현대 연극의 주인공 _____

05. 습관은 물려진다. _____

06. 우리는 동물과는 다르다. _____

C A의 단어를 활용하여 다음 문장의 빈칸에 문맥상 알맞은 말을 쓰시오.

01. This _____ book is thoughtful and informative as well as fascinating.

02. A(n) _____ is an optical instrument used to magnify and enhance the view of faraway objects.

03. A(n) _____ is a tool that lets the user see objects at a magnification greater than the actual specimen.

04. If you are _____ for an examination, you are learning as much as possible in a short time just before you take the examination.

05. To _____ a situation means to be the most powerful or important person or thing in it.

06. _____ was excluded as a planet because it did not dominate its surroundings or obtain its round shape due to the force of its own gravity.

D 다음 문장의 빈칸에 어법상 알맞은 것을 고르시오.

01. One day he disappeared from the city, _____ .
   ① never to be seen   ② to never be seen   ③ to be never seen

02. The room is _____ a library.
   ① as absolutely quiet as   ② as absolute quiet as   ③ as quiet absolutely as

03. _____ anything new, you have to have an open mind.
   ① In order for learn   ② In order for learning   ③ In order to learn

04. The hole in the kitchen is _____ that in my room. (더욱 더 깊다)
   ① more deeper than   ② even deeper than   ③ less deeper than

05. Some reptiles change skin color _____ to their surroundings.
   ① so as themselves adapt   ② as so to adapt themselves
   ③ so as to adapt themselves

06. She got him _____ .
   ① clean up the mess   ② to clean up the mess   ③ to cleaning up the mess

07. This tool is _____ that tool. (덜 유용하지 않다.)
   ① not less useful than   ② not more useful than   ③ less useful than

08. Did you think _____ ?
   ① the exam being difficult   ② the exam difficult   ③ difficult the exam

09. _____ , you must first be a good friend.
   ① Having made good friends ② To make good friends ③ Making good friends

10. They called _____ .
   ① his sister as a professor   ② his sister a professor   ③ his sister to be a professor

Chapter 04

알고 있는 단어에 체크하고 단어들의 뜻을 쓰시오.

active

acute

astronomer

bark

compound

conscious

contract

craft

demonstrate

disorder

diverse

drastic

dyeing

effect *v.*

emission

emit

endeavor

eventually

expand

expertise

fabric

fungus

hydrogen

hypnosis

hypnotherapy

illuminate

inevitably

ingredient

irritate

lighthearted

liken

manufacture

microbe

nebula

nitrogen

oxygen

paralysis

pay attention to

penetrate

pharmaceutical

planetary

potential

prevail

prevalent

psychologically

relieve

remnant

represent

rheumatism

snowflake

subconscious

suspect

synonymous

synthesize

take up

trance

trick *n.*

ultraviolet

weaving

willow

The magician asks a member of the audience to join him on stage for his next trick, hypnotizing someone so that he or she will do something funny. The audience member feeling he or she cannot be hypnotized jumps on the stage. Inevitably the magician prevails. The person falling into a hypnotic trance speaks and possibly reveals something best left unrevealed. Since he is a magician, are we to think that hypnosis is a form of magic? Or is hypnosis a scientific endeavor? Perhaps it is a combination of both these things.

Psychologically speaking, hypnotherapy is a proven method of treating various psychological disorders. It can be used to control our brains so that we alter our behavior. Research has shown that the conscious mind is controlled by our unconscious mind, which is really the driving force behind all our thoughts and behaviors. Hypnosis is a scientific method which allows us to enter the subconscious in order to reprogram desires and effect behavior changes.

Hypnosis is also part <u>art</u> because it can be learned through practice as magic can. Hypnosis has been likened to playing a musical instrument. While we may have a talent to hypnotize, we will never be able to actually do it unless we practice it. Hypnotherapy is also a craft because individuals with the expertise can use it for lighthearted entertainment. Stage hypnosis is practiced successfully by many professionals, who manage to make people laugh even while demonstrating how powerful our subconscious really is.

Words

- hypnotize [hípnətàiz] ~에게 최면을 걸다 • inevitably [inévitəbli] 불가피하게, 확실히 • prevail [privéil] 우세하다, 이기다
- hypnotic [hipnátik] 최면의 • trance [træns] 혼수상태 • hypnosis [hipnóusis] 최면(술) • endeavor [endévər] 노력, 시도
- hypnotherapy [hìpnouθérəpi] 최면요법 • disorder [disɔ́:rdər] 장애, 이상 • subconscious [sʌbkánʃəs] 잠재의식(의)
- effect [ifékt] 초래하다, 가져오다 • liken [láikən] 비유하다, 견주다 • craft [kræft] 기술 • expertise [èkspərtíːz] 전문 기술
- lighthearted [láithá:rtid] 쾌활한, 마음 편한

Info Scan

1. Which of the following is NOT correct? (choose two)

① Hypnosis can be used to treat people with various mental problems.

② Hypnosis is merely a trick which some skilled people can play.

③ Anyone can pick up the ability to hypnotize someone through exercises.

④ Hypnosis deals with our subconscious mind that can affect our behaviour.

⑤ Many scientists hesitate to accept hypnosis as part of any scientific field.

Vocabulary

2. 밑줄 친 art와 같은 뜻으로 사용된 단어 두 개를 본문에서 찾아 쓰시오.

....

....

Analysis

3. 최면술이 art이기도 한 두 가지 이유를 우리말로 설명하시오.

....

....

Inference

4. Which of the following can be inferred from the passage?

① It is almost impossible for an ordinary person to master hypnosis.

② Hypnosis can be either a science or a craft depending on how it is used.

③ Even novices can succeed in hypnotizing people after several attempts.

④ Hypnosis is practiced in various fields of medical science in many countries.

⑤ Hypnosis is mainly used to enter the subconscious in criminal investigations.

Grammar be to 용법

- Since he is a magician, are we to think that hypnosis is a form of magic? ⋯ 가능
- The concert is to be held this evening. ⋯ 예정
- He was never to see his family again. ⋯ 운명
- You are to knock before you come in. ⋯ 의무
- This camera was not to be found. ⋯ 가능
- If you are to succeed, you must work hard. ⋯ 의도

Tips to부정사가 be동사 뒤에 쓰일 때, be to 용법이라 하며 〈예정, 운명, 의무, 가능, 의도〉의 내용을 표현한다. 이 때 to부정사는 형용사적 용법이라는 데에 주의한다.

▌ Quiz 다음을 영작하고 be to 용법 중 어디에 속하는지 쓰시오.

1. 너는 이 방에서 떠들면 안 된다. → You _____ in this room. 〈   〉
2. 그녀는 치명적인 사고 이후 결코 걷지 못할 것이었다. → She _____ after the accident. 〈   〉

Structure 분사구의 명사 수식

The person falling into a hypnotic trance speaks and possibly reveals something best left unrevealed.

◎ The person이란 어떤 사람을 말하는가?

→ _____ (해석)

◎ something이란 어떤 것인가?

→ _____ (해석)

문장의 구조	주어 + 동사 + 목적어

- 주어 → ....
- 동사 → ....
- 목적어 → ....

다음 밑줄 친 우리말을 문맥에 맞게 영작하시오.

1. The magician asks a member of the audience to join him on stage
   for his next trick, hypnotizing someone 그 또는 그녀가 재미있는 무언가를
   할 수 있도록.

   ↳

2. It 조절하는 데에 사용될 수 있다 our brains so that we alter our behavior.

   ↳

3. Hypnosis is a scientific method which 우리를 ~로 들어가게 하다 the
   subconscious in order to reprogram desires and effect behavior
   changes.

   ↳

4. Hypnosis 연주하는 것에 비유되어 왔다 a musical instrument.

   ↳

5. Many professionals manage to make people laugh even while
   demonstrating 우리의 잠재의식이 정말 얼마나 강력한지.

   ↳

Born in 1825, Friedrich Bayer was one of six children in his family. Bayer took up his father's trade, dyeing and weaving, and started a successful dye business of his own in 1848. After the discovery of coal-tar based dyes in 1856, Bayer and another master dyer, Friedrich Weskott, formed the Friedrich Bayer Company to manufacture such dyes since they thought such dyes had great commercial potential.

(A)

While it relieved pain, the powder form of aspirin, salicylic acid, irritated the drug taker's stomach and mouth. This side effect was not solved until Hoffmann, on August 10, 1897, produced a chemically pure type of acetyl salicylic acid. The Bayer Company thus became _____ the drug aspirin.

(B)

When Bayer died on May 6, 1880, the company was involved principally in the fabric dye business. After Bayer's death the company continued to hire chemists to invent new dyes and other products which were based on the new dyes.

(C)

In 1897, one of the Friedrich Bayer Company's chemists, Felix Hoffmann, conducted experiments with some of the various chemicals used in the dyes to try to find a drug which would help his father deal with the medical condition of rheumatism. Eventually a stable form of salicylic acid which came from the bark of the willow tree was chemically synthesized by Hoffman. The compound became the active ingredient in a pharmaceutical wonder product: Aspirin. The "a" came from acetyl, and the "spir" came from the spirea plant, which salicin comes from.

Words

- dyeing [dáiiŋ] 염색 • weaving [wíːviŋ] 직조 • dye [dai] 염료, 염색하다 • coal-tar [kóultɑːr] 콜타르
- salicylic acid 살리실산 • irritate [írətèit] 염증을 일으키다 • side effect 부작용 • not ~ until …하고 나서야 ~하다
- acetyl [əsíːtil] 아세틸 • fabric [fǽbrik] 직물 • rheumatism [rúːmətìzəm] 류머티즘 • bark [ɑːrk] 껍질
- willow [wílou] 버드나무 • synthesize [sínθəsàiz] 합성하다 • active [ǽktiv] 특효 있는
- pharmaceutical [fɑ̀ːrməsúːtikəl] 제약의 • spirea [spairíːə] 조팝나뭇과의 관목

Coherence

1. 글의 흐름이 자연스럽도록 (A), (B), (C)의 순서를 바르게 배열한 것은?

① (A) - (C) - (B)
② (B) - (A) - (C)
③ (B) - (C) - (A)
④ (C) - (A) - (B)
⑤ (C) - (B) - (A)

Detail

2. Felix Hoffmann이 아스피린을 연구하게 된 최초 이유를 우리말로 설명하시오.

....

Coherence

3. 빈칸에 들어갈 알맞은 말은?

① dependent on
② influential in
③ synonymous with
④ well off
⑤ patented

Info Scan

4. Which of the following is correct according to the passage?

① The name Aspirin came from the first inventor of the drug.
② Friedrich Bayer devoted his life to the invention of Aspirin.
③ There were many people participated in creating Aspirin.
④ Aspirin was first invented by one of Bayer's scientists.
⑤ Hofmann couldn't figure out what had caused the side effect.

Grammar   수동태

- This side effect was not solved.
- The company was involved principally in the fabric dye business.
- A stable form of salicylic acid was chemically synthesized by Hoffman.

Tips 동작을 행하는 주체와 그 동작을 받는 대상이 있을 때, 능동태는 동작을 행하는 주체를 주어로 삼고, 수동태는 동작을 받는
대상을 주어로 삼는다.

| Quiz   다음을 영작하시오.

1. 그 책은 쉬운 영어로 쓰여 있어서, 읽기가 쉬웠다.
   → As the book _____ easy English, it is easy to read.

2. 이 꽃은 '장미' 라고 우리에 의해 불린다.   → This flower _____.

Structure   형용사절의 명사 수식

Eventually a stable form of salicylic acid which came from the bark of the willow tree was chemically synthesized by Hoffman.

◯ 살리실산(salicylic acid)은 어디서 구한 것인가?

　→

　→ (해석)

◯ Eventually가 수식하는 것은?

　→

문장의 구조	(문장 부사) + 주어 + 동사 + 보어 + (전치사구)

- (문장 부사) → ....
- 주어　→ ....
- 동사　→ ....
- 보어　→ ....
- (전치사구) → ....

* 수동태의 〈be동사+과거분사〉를 2형식의 〈be동사+보어〉로 간주한다.

Writing

다음 밑줄 친 우리말을 문맥에 맞게 영작하시오.

1. 그것이 통증을 가라앉히는 동안, the powder form of aspirin, salicylic acid, irritated the drug taker's stomach and mouth.

   └→
   ....

2. This side effect ~할 때까지 해결되지 않았다 Hoffmann, on August 10, 1897, produced a chemically pure type of acetyl salicylic acid.

   └→
   ....

3. Felix Hoffmann ~을 가지고 실험을 했다 some of the various chemicals used in the dyes to try to find a drug.

   └→
   ....

4. A drug would 그의 아버지가 ~을 치료하도록 돕다 the medical condition of rheumatism.

   └→
   ....

5. Eventually a stable form of salicylic acid which came from the bark of the willow tree ~에 의해서 화학적으로 합성되었다 Hoffman.

   └→
   ....

As stars burn out they emit glowing gases, which make colorful and complex shapes when viewed by powerful telescopes such as the Hubble Space Telescope. These emissions or gaseous clouds are known as planetary nebulae. Originally viewed in the eighteenth century through small and less powerful telescopes, astronomers thought the round shape of these gaseous clouds looked like the other planets in the solar system.

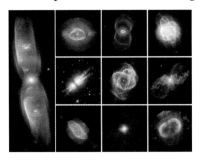

Planetary nebulae are produced when stars in their final stages of life shed their top layers of material. This material turns into gaseous clouds which are illuminated by ultraviolet light from the remnant star. These glowing gaseous clouds last for about a few tens of thousands of years, which is not a long time considering such sun-like stars usually have a lifespan of over 10 billion years. As time passes these gaseous clouds expand and become larger. Furthermore, as time passes the ultraviolet light penetrates more deeply into the gas, causing the nebulae to glow more brightly.

Modern images of planetary nebulae show how they expand and contract in varied size as well as in temperature. In terms of their shape, nebulae are actually like snowflakes, showing an incredibly diverse and complex range of shapes. The relatively youthful nebula is quite small and is surrounded by nitrogen gas. Each color represents a different kind of gas being emitted. Nitrogen produces red light; hydrogen produces green light; and oxygen produces blue light.

Words

- emit [imít] 발산하다 • planetary [plǽnətèri] 행성의 • nebula [nébjələ] 성운 (pl. nebulae) • astronomer [əstránəmər] 천문학자
- illuminate [ilú:mənèit] 비추다, 광채를 더하다 • ultraviolet [Àltrəváiəlit] 자외선 • remnant [rémnənt] 잔존물, 나머지
- penetrate [pénətrèit] 침투하다, 관통하다 • contract [kántrækt] 수축하다 • in terms of ~의 점에서 보면
- nitrogen [náitrədʒən] 질소 • hydrogen [háidrədʒən] 수소 • oxygen [áksidʒən] 산소

Coherence

1. 빈칸에 들어갈 알맞은 문장은?

① Thus the name planetary nebula was used among only a few people.

② But the planetary nebulae were renamed after recent images.

③ But the name planetary nebulae weren't given in the eighteenth century.

④ As the name planetary nebula represents, it is a type of planets.

⑤ But, in fact, the planetary nebula has nothing to do with planets.

Info Scan

2. Which of the following is NOT true about planetary nebulae?

① They consist of a glowing shell of gas formed at the end of stars' lives.

② The name originated from the similarity in appearance to the other planets.

③ They gather together and eventually become big enough to form a star.

④ Advanced telescopes revealed that they have complex and varied shapes.

⑤ They are a relatively short-lived phenomenon, lasting over 10,000 years.

Detail

3. snowflakes와 planetary nebulae은 어떤 점에서 비슷한지를 우리말로 쓰시오.

....

Analysis

4. 붉은빛을 내는 planetary nebula를 통해 우리가 추측할 수 있는 것 세 가지를 쓰시오.

....

....

....

Grammar 분사구문 – 현재분사와 과거분사

- Originally viewed in the eighteenth century, astronomers thought the round shape of these gaseous clouds looked like the other planets.
- The ultraviolet light penetrates more deeply into the gas, causing the nebulae to glow more brightly.

Tips 분사구문이란 〈접속사 + 주어 + 동사〉의 부사절에서 접속사와 주어를 생략하고 현재분사나 과거분사를 이용해 부사구로 바꾼 것이다. 접속사를 생략하고, 주절의 주어와 같을 경우 주어까지 생략하고 부사절의 동사를 현재분사로 바꾸면 된다. 한편, Being이나 Having been으로 시작하는 경우에는 Being이나 Having been을 생략해서, 과거분사구문이 된다.

▌Quiz 다음 문장을 분사구문으로 바꾸어 쓰시오.

1. As I have read the newspaper, I know about the accident.
   → _____ , I know about the accident.
2. As it was fine, we went on a picnic. → _____ , we went on a picnic.

Structure 형용사절의 명사 수식

These glowing gaseous clouds last for about a few tens of thousands of years, which is not a long time considering such sun-like stars usually have a lifespan of over 10 billion years.

◯ which의 선행사는?

   → ....

◯ considering 다음에 생략된 말을 쓰고, 이를 if절로 바꾸어 쓰시오.

   → considering
   → If
   → (해석)

문장의 구조	주어 + 동사 + (전치사구) + (관계사절) + (분사구)

- 주어 → ....
- 동사 → ....
- (전치사구) → ....

- (관계사절) → ....
- (분사구) → ....

Writing

다음 밑줄 친 우리말을 문맥에 맞게 영작하시오.

1. The planetary nebula ~과 관련이 없다 planets.

   └

2. These glowing gaseous clouds ~동안 지속된다 about a few tens of thousands of years.

   └

3. It ~을 고려하면 긴 시간은 아니다 such sun-like stars usually have a lifespan of over 10 billion years.

   └

4. As time passes the ultraviolet light penetrates more deeply into the gas, 그 성운을 더 밝게 타오르게 하면서.

   └

5. 그것들의 모양으로 보면, nebulae are actually like snowflakes, showing an incredibly diverse and complex range of shapes.

   └

Honeybees are disappearing for unknown reasons around the United States. The decline has been drastic: In 2006, 23 percent of honeybees kept by beekeepers disappeared. Scientists are trying to come up with a possible explanation for the bee decline, also called Colony Collapse Disorder. Scientists first looked for evidence of microbes living only in the sick colonies. Two types of fungi were suspected of causing Colony Collapse Disorder. And another suspect was a little-known virus called Israeli Acute Paralysis Virus (IAPV).

Researchers have been studying bee colonies in which the bees have been disappearing and comparing those colonies to colonies in which the bees have not been disappearing. At first researchers thought the prime suspects were two types of fungi, but then they discovered that these fungi were prevalent in not only the colonies experiencing Colony Collapse Disorder but also colonies which were not experiencing this disorder.

The IAPV virus, however, showed up in 83 percent of the colonies experiencing Colony Collapse Disorder. Only 5 percent of the colonies not experiencing this disorder had the presence of this virus in their colonies. In 2004, researchers in Israel first claimed that the virus kills bees. But until now, bee experts haven't paid much attention to it. But they now know that the presence of IAPV is a strong sign that a colony has the disorder. Scientists are not sure whether IAPV can single-handedly cause Colony Collapse Disorder, so they are continuing their research to try to find out what other factors might be involved in this process. They also want to find out how IAPV came to the United States. Currently bee products are being imported from Canada, Australia, and New Zealand. However, if it turns out that this trade is spreading disease, the rules might eventually change.

Words

• drastic [dræstik] 격렬한, 강렬한   • beekeeper [bíːkìːpər] 양봉업자   • Colony Collapse Disorder 군집 붕괴 현상
• microbe [máikròub] 미생물, 세균   • suspect [səspékt] 의심(하다)   • Israeli Acute Paralysis Virus 이스라엘 급성 마비 바이러스
• fungus [fʌ́ŋgəs] 버섯, 균류   • prevalent [prévələnt] 널리 보급된   • pay attention to ~에 주의를 기울이다   • turn out 판명되다

Info Scan **1.** Which of the following is NOT true about bee decline? (choose two)

① Scientists think IAPV may not be the only reason for the decline.
② The virus has been found in imported bees and bee products.
③ Scientists first suspected two types of fungi were the cause.
④ Scientists have found a reasonable solution for the bee decline.
⑤ The number of bees in U.S. has decreased tremendously.

Analysis **2.** 다음 빈칸에 colony 수의 정도를 넣어 Colony Collapse Disorder에 대한 실험 결과를 나타내시오. (many, some, a few, zero 등)

• Fungi : in .... colonies with symptoms

in .... colonies without symptoms

• IAPV : in .... colonies with symptoms

in .... colonies without symptoms

Inference **3.** Which of the following can be inferred from the passage?

① The bees from other countries will be banned.
② The case is not completely concluded yet.
③ Bee population in the U.S. will increase again.
④ Scientists will find a way to remove the virus.
⑤ The research on bee decline started in 2004.

Analysis **4.** 현재 IAPV에 대해 진행되고 있는 두 가지의 연구를 쓰시오.

....

....

Grammar 시제 일치의 예외

- In 2004, researchers in Israel first claimed that the virus kills bees.
- ⁺ He said that Columbus discovered America in 1492.
- ⁺ If it is fine tomorrow, we will go on a picnic.

Tips 주절의 동사가 현재에서 과거로 바뀌어도 종속절의 시제가 변하지 않는 경우가 있다. 첫째, 종속절이 불변의 진리인 경우에는 항상 현재로만 쓴다. 둘째, 현재까지 계속되는 습관적 행위는 현재시제로 쓴다. 셋째, 역사적 사실은 과거시제로만 쓴다. 넷째, 시간과 조건의 부사절에서는 미래시제 대신에 현재시제를 쓴다.

❙ Quiz 다음을 영작하시오.

1. 만약 그녀를 다시 만나게 되면 나는 그녀에게 진실을 말할 것이다. → I will tell her the truth _____.

2. 내가 다시 사회적으로 활동적인 사람이 될 수나 있을지 궁금하다. (ever)
   → I wonder if I _____ socially active again.

Structure 형용사절의 명사 수식

Researchers have been studying <u>bee colonies</u> in which the bees have been disappearing and comparing those colonies to <u>colonies</u> in which the bees have not been disappearing.

❍ 밑줄 친 bee colonies란 어떤 colonies를 말하는가?

→ _____

❍ comparing 앞에 생략된 말은?

→ _____

❍ 밑줄 친 colonies란 어떤 colonies인가?

→ _____

문장의 구조	주어 + 동사 + 목적어 + 연결어 and + 동사 + 목적어 + (전치사구)

- 주어 → ....
- 동사 → ....
- 목적어 → ....
- 연결어 → and

- 동사 → ....
- 목적어 → ....
- (전치사구) → ....

Writing

다음 밑줄 친 우리말을 문맥에 맞게 영작하시오.

1. Scientists ~을 찾아내기 위해 노력하고 있다 a possible explanation for the bee decline.

   └→

2. Researchers ~을 비교해오고 있다 those colonies to colonies in which the bees have not been disappearing.

   └→

3. Only 5 percent of the colonies 이런 병을 겪지 않은 had the presence of this virus in their colonies.

   └→

4. In 2004, researchers in Israel first 그 바이러스가 벌들을 죽인다고 주장했다.

   └→

5. So they are continuing their research to try to find out 어떤 다른 요소들 이 관련이 있을지 in this process.

   └→

Review

A   다음 단어의 뜻을 쓰시오.

01. diverse _____   07. pharmaceutical _____

02. emit _____   08. prevail _____

03. illuminate _____ 09. stable _____

04. nebula _____   10. subconscious _____

05. oxygen _____   11. synonymous _____

06. penetrate _____   12. trance _____

B   A의 단어를 활용하여 다음 우리말에 맞게 영작하시오.

01. 혼수상태에 빠지다 _____

02. 제약 회사 _____

03. 열, 빛이나 가스를 발산하다 _____

04. 잠재의식의 숨겨진 힘 _____

05. 유가는 안정되어야 한다. (remain) _____

06. Security는 Safety와 동의어이다. _____

C   A의 단어를 활용하여 다음 문장의 빈칸에 문맥상 알맞은 말을 쓰시오.

01. To _____ something means to shine light on it and to make it brighter and more visible.

02. If something or someone _____ a physical object or an area, it succeeds in getting into or passing through the object or area.

03. Water consists of one _____ atom and two hydrogen atoms.

04. "_____" comes from the Latin word for cloud or dust. The word "nebulae" is the plural form.

05. If a group or range of things is _____, it is made up of a wide variety of things.

06. If a proposal, principle, or opinion _____, it gains influence or is accepted, often after a struggle or argument.

D 다음 문장의 빈칸에 어법상 알맞은 것을 고르시오.

01. We _____ the gallery to see the exhibition of Vincent Van Gogh tomorrow.
① goes to ② went to ③ are to go to

02. The Science teacher told us that the Earth _____ the sun.
① moved around ② will move around ③ moves around

03. The problems that the participants had _____.
① have settled ② been settled ③ were settled

04. Those who didn't hand in the assignment _____ poorly.
① will grade ② will be graded ③ to be graded

05. My boyfriend said that he _____ every morning.
① will take a walk ② takes a walk ③ took a walk

06. _____ at a bargain, you'd better drop by the flea market.
① If you can buy it ② If you are to buy it ③ If you buy it

07. _____ in better times, he would have become famous.
① Having been born ② Bearing ③ Having born

08. The meeting _____ in 10 minutes.
① is to be held ② will be to be held ③ has been held

09. I will tell her the truth _____ again.
① I will see her ② if I saw her ③ if I see her

10. _____ the news, I called him to see if he was okay or not.
① To hear ② Having heard ③ To be heard

Chapter 05

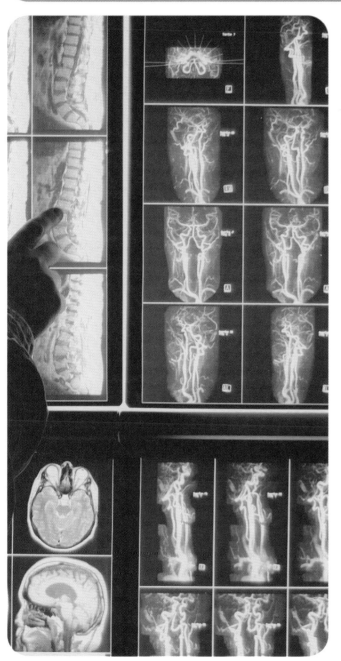

Vocabulary Pre-check

알고 있는 단어에 체크하고 단어들의 뜻을 쓰시오.

- affect
- assurance
- at least
- awkwardly
- bipolar
- breed
- capacity
- cattle
- clinically
- command
- composition
- concentrate
- depression
- diplomatic
- ecstatic
- estimate
- excitable
- extinction
- extreme
- fatal
- figure *n.*
- get around
- hind feet
- hybrid
- impair
- impressive
- indicate
- inevitably
- justify
- lay
- manic-depressive
- marinated
- mating season
- membrane
- normalization
- occupy
- outweigh
- photographic memory
- possess
- pros and cons
- regarding
- regulator
- reproduce
- revelation
- shallow
- skeptical
- spade-like
- standard
- strain
- sufficient
- swing
- territory
- unidentifiable
- use up

Since it lives in the dry hot desert, the Spadefoot Toad, which has long, pointy spade-like hind feet, has been forced to adapt for its survival. The dry weather causes special problems during the mating season. Females lay their eggs in pools of water, but if the pools dry up before the tadpoles become toads, the Spadefoot Toad might face extinction since tadpoles cannot live on dry land as toads can.

A new study shows that spadefoot parents get around this problem in a very unusual way. Most animal species don't breed with one another, and spadefoots generally don't either. But they will during dry seasons if it helps their young survive. Two spadefoot species, Spea bombifrons and Spea multiplicata, both live in the southwestern United States, where they often occupy the same territory. They can mate with each other, though there are pros and cons to doing so.

On the one side for S. bombifrons, the hybrid tadpoles develop faster than tadpoles with two S. bombifrons parents. The hybrid tadpoles are therefore more likely to survive if they are born in a shallow pool that dries up quickly. On the other side, the hybrids tend to have problems reproducing once they become adults. Scientists have discovered that when S. bombifrons females are breeding in particularly shallow pools, they seem to decide that the pros of breeding with the other species outweigh the cons.

Words

- **Spadefoot Toad** 쟁기발두꺼비   • **spade-like** [speidlaik] 쟁기모양의   • **hind feet** 뒷다리   • **adapt** [ədǽpt] 적합하다, 적응하다
- **lay** [lei] (알을) 낳다   • **tadpole** [tǽdpòul] 올챙이   • **extinction** [ikstíŋkʃən] 멸종   • **get around** 이겨내다, 헤어나다
- **breed** [briːd] 번식시키다, 낳다   • **territory** [térətɔ̀ːri] 영토   • **pros and cons** 장단점, 찬반양론   • **hybrid** [háibrid] 혼혈의
- **shallow** [ʃǽlou] 얕은   • **tend to** ~하는 경향이 있다   • **reproduce** [rìːprədjúːs] 번식하다, 생식하다
- **outweigh** [àutwéi] ~보다 가치가 있다, 중요하다

Info Scan

1. Which of the following is true?

① Spadefoot toads would not lay their eggs in shallow water.
② Spadefoot toads strictly mate within limited kinds of species.
③ Tadpoles will adapt to survive on land during the dry season.
④ Different species of spadefoot toad can live in the same area.
⑤ Many spadefoot toad species are facing the threat of extinction.

Summary

2. 다음 빈칸을 완성하여 관찰 결과를 완성하시오.

➜ S. bombifrons females will break the usual rule and mate
with _____ in order to produce
_____ that will hop out of those shallow
pools before _____.

Analysis

3. Explain the pros and cons of mating with a different species in Korean.

• pros: ....

• cons: ....

Vocabulary

4. 밑줄 친 occupy와 의미상 가장 가까운 것은?

① clear   ② divide
③ inhabit   ④ reproduce
⑤ fight for

Grammar lay와 lie의 구분

• Females lay their eggs in pools of water. 암컷은 물 웅덩이에 알을 낳는다.

+ He lay down on the grass. 그는 풀밭에 드러누웠다.

+ He lied about his age. 그는 자기 나이를 속였다.

Tips lay와 lie를 잘 구분해야 한다. 의미뿐 아니라 과거, 과거분사 변화형에도 주의한다. 우선 lay는 타동사로서「눕히다, 놓다, (알을) 낳다」라는 뜻이며, 그 변화형은 lay-laid-laid-laying이다. lie는 자동사인데,「눕다, 드러눕다, 누워 있다」의 의미일 때는 lie-lay-lain-lying의 변화형을 가지며,「거짓말하다」의 의미일 때는 lie-lied-lied-lying의 형태로 변한다.

┃ Quiz 다음 괄호 안에서 알맞은 것을 고르시오.

1. You're [lying / laying] to me.

2. The dog was [lying / laying] on the ground.

3. I saw the book [laid / lain / lied] on the table.

4. The great ocean of truth [lay / laid / lied] undiscovered before me.

Structure 관계부사절

Two spadefoot species, Spea bombifrons and Spea multiplicata, both live in the southwestern United States, where they often occupy the same territory.

◎ Two spadefoot species와 동격인 것은?

→ ....

◎ where의 선행사는?

→ ....

문장의 구조	주어 + 동사 + (전치사구) + (관계부사절)

• 주어 → .... • (전치사구) → ....

• 동사 → .... • (관계부사절) → ....

Writing

다음 밑줄 친 우리말을 문맥에 맞게 영작하시오.

1. The Spadefoot Toad might face extinction since tadpoles cannot live on dry land 두꺼비가 그럴 수 있는 것처럼.

    └,

2. Spadefoot parents 이 문제를 이겨낸다 in a very unusual way.

    └,

3. They will during dry seasons 그것이 어린 것들을 살아남게 하는 데에 도움이 된다면.

    └,

4. The hybrid tadpoles 그래서 더 ~하게 될 것 같다 survive if they are born in a shallow pool that dries up quickly.

    └,

5. On the other side, the hybrids 번식하는 데에 문제를 가지게 되는 경향이 있다 once they become adults.

    └,

Everyone experiences mood swings at times, but some people have such extreme mood swings that they are clinically ill. These people can feel ecstatic for a few weeks about something happening to them that would merely be pleasant to someone else. (A) Then they can shift into a severe depression, being unable to concentrate and having extremely negative thoughts about themselves. (B) The cause for the depression might be unidentifiable. (C)

In many cases such extreme mood swings indicate that the person is suffering from one of two forms of bipolar illness. (D) The first type of bipolar illness, bipolar I disorder, was previously called manic-depressive illness. (E) People who suffer from this illness go through either periods of mania, extreme happiness, and then depression or simply go through only a period of mania or depression. People who are experiencing bipolar I disorder have trouble relating to others because of their disorder. To be considered to be going through an episode of depression, the period of depression must last at least two weeks, but a clinical definition of mania doesn't require that a person feel ecstatic for any set period of time.

Patients suffering from bipolar II disorder which usually starts with a depressive episode have mainly depression and a few manic episodes. They are not as socially impaired in their interactions with others as patients suffering from bipolar I disorder. They carry on in their daily life and with their daily routines.

Words

• swing [swiŋ] 변동, 동요 • clinically [klínikəli] 임상적으로 • unidentifiable [ənaidéntəfàiəbəl] 확인될 수 없는
• indicate [índikèit] 가리키다, 지적하다 • bipolar [baipóulər] 쌍극성의 • manic-depressive [mǽnikdiprésiv] 조울증의
• mania [méiniə] 조병(躁病); 열중 • at least 적어도 • impair [impέər] 손상하다, 해치다

Info Scan **1.** According to the passage, which of the following is true? (choose two)

① Bipolar disorder can be divided into two types depending on its symptoms.

② Bipolar disorder can be diagnosed and treated easily without any aftereffects.

③ The symptoms of bipolar disorder are very similar to regular mood swings.

④ Patients with bipolar disorder can have uplifted moods and depression by turns.

⑤ People with bipolar disorder always have same periods of mania and depression.

Analysis **2.** 다음 증상을 보고 bipolar I인지 bipolar II인지를 구분하여 쓰시오.

- .... 사람들과의 관계가 어렵다.
- .... 심한 흥분과 우울이 반복된다.
- .... 사람들과의 관계가 손상되지 않는다.
- .... 흥분하는 경우는 적고 주로 우울만 계속된다.

Coherence **3.** 글의 흐름상 주어진 문장이 들어가기 적절한 곳은?

If it is known, it is clear that most people would not react this deeply to this kind of problem.

① (A)   ② (B)   ③ (C)

④ (D)   ⑤ (E)

Vocabulary **4.** 밑줄 친 ecstatic과 같은 의미로 사용된 단어를 본문에서 찾아 쓰시오.

....

Grammar   형용사 보어

- These people can *feel* ecstatic for a few weeks.
- ⁺ The little child *looked* pale.

Tips 보어는 사람이나 사물의 상태를 설명한다. 주격보어와 목적격보어가 있다. 이런 보어 자리에 올 수 있는 것은 명사, 형용사 등이다. 부사가 올 수 없다는 데에 유의해야 한다.

❙ Quiz   다음 문장에서 어색한 부분을 찾아 고쳐 쓰시오.

1. Good medicine tastes bitterly. → _____

2. The lake looks beautifully in the moonlight. → _____

Structure   분사구의 명사 수식

Patients suffering from bipolar II disorder which usually starts with a depressive episode have mainly depression and a few manic episodes.

◎ Patients란 어떤 사람들인가?

→ ....

◎ bipolar II disorder란 어떠한 병인가?

→ ....

문장의 구조	주어 + 동사 + 목적어

- 주어   → ....
- 동사   → ....
- 목적어 → ....

Writing

다음 밑줄 친 우리말을 문맥에 맞게 영작하시오.

1. These people can feel ecstatic 그들에게 일어나는 것에 대해 that would merely be pleasant to someone else.

2. The cause for the depression 확인되지 않을지도 모른다.

3. People who are experiencing bipolar I disorder ~와 관계를 맺는 데에 문제가 있다 others because of their disorder.

4. The period of depression 적어도 2주간 지속되어야 한다.

5. They are not as socially impaired ~와 상호작용을 하는 데에 있어서 others as patients suffering from bipolar I disorder.

A single case of mad cow disease in December of 2003 has greatly affected the trading relationship between Korea and America. Americans have been pushing for the normalization of beef trade, but Koreans have been concerned about their health.

After all, mad cow disease is fatal and public fears are not easily pushed aside by the assurances of government regulators. Defining 'normalization' is not an easy thing to do, but Korea is following international standards regarding the safety and importation of American beef these days. (A) Nevertheless, it is clear that the revelation in December of 2003 that one American cow had mad cow disease will inevitably continue to strain diplomatic relationships. (B)

Scientists tell the public that by eating infected beef they can get the same disease cows have. So citizens cannot put a burger to their lips without wondering if the beef patty will make them go crazy. (C) Furthermore, housewives now carefully check the origin of beef they buy in the supermarket. (D) And people think that cheap prices for marinated beef ribs in restaurants must mean they have been imported from America. So, you ought to think twice before eating there. (E)

The origin of this skeptical behavior is the horrible nature of the disease itself. Cattle infected with this disease exhibit odd and strange behavior. They seem to be constantly stressed and nervous. They fall down unexpectedly and walk awkwardly. The reason is that the animals' brain and central nervous system are being broken down by the disease. And because the disease has the same effect on humans, well, our doubts seem justified.

Words

- mad cow disease 광우병 • push for ~을 자꾸 요구하다 • normalization [nɔ̀ːrməlizéiʃən] 정상화
- regulator [régjəlèitər] 규정자, 단속자 • regarding [rigáːrdiŋ] ~에 관한 • revelation [rèvəléiʃən] 폭로, 의외의 일
- strain [strein] 긴장시키다 • diplomatic [dìpləmǽtik] 외교의 • not ~ without doing ~하면 반드시 …하다
- marinated [mǽrinèitid] 양념된 • skeptical [sképtikəl] 의심 많은, 회의적인 • cattle [kǽtl] (집합적) 소, 가축

Coherence

1. 글의 흐름상 주어진 문장이 들어가기 가장 적절한 곳은?

> The stress results partly from the public's fears about health.

① (A) ② (B) ③ (C)
④ (D) ⑤ (E)

Vocabulary

2. 밑줄 친 inevitably의 의미와 가장 가까운 것은?

① finally ② eventually
③ unavoidably ④ certainly
⑤ gradually

Analysis

3. 밑줄 친 this skeptical behavior가 가리키는 행동으로, 본문에 언급된 세 가지를 우리말로 쓰시오.

....

....

....

Info Scan

4. According to the passage, which of the following is true? (choose two)

① There have been many cases of mad cow disease in the United States.
② The U.S. government has succeeded in normalizing beef export.
③ The disease can be transferred to a person who eats infected beef.
④ Korean people became very hesitant about buying imported beef.
⑤ Mad cow disease has been found in beef imported from many countries.

Grammar 집합명사와 군집명사

- Cattle infected with this disease exhibit odd and strange behavior.
- + The police are after him.

Tips 집합명사란 집합체(단체)를 나타내는 명사로서 단수형과 복수형이 있다. 군집명사는 집합체의 개체(구성원)들을 나타내는 명사로서 형태는 단수형이지만 내용상 복수로 취급한다. cattle, vermin, poultry 등은 부정관사를 붙이지 못하고 복수형으로 쓰일 수 없다. furniture, clothing 등은 관사 없이 항상 단수형으로 쓰며 단수로 취급한다. police, clergy는 정관사와 함께 쓰고 항상 단수형이며 복수로 취급된다.

| Quiz 다음을 영작하시오.

1. 내 방에는 가구가 거의 없다. → I have ＿＿＿＿＿＿＿＿＿＿＿＿ in my room.

2. 성직자들은 그 회의에 참석했다. (clergy, be present) → ＿＿＿＿＿＿＿＿＿＿＿＿ at the meeting.

3. 가금류는 사람이 먹을 식량으로 고기와 달걀을 제공하기 위해 사육되는 조류이다. (poultry)
   → ＿＿＿＿＿＿＿＿＿＿＿＿ that are raised to provide meat and eggs for human food.

Structure 동격

The revelation in December of 2003 that one American cow had mad cow disease will inevitably continue to strain diplomatic relationships.

◎ The revelation이란 어떤 내용인가?
- → (어떤 내용)
- → (해석)

문장의 구조	주어 + (전치사구) + (동격절) + 동사 + 목적어

- 주어 → ＿＿＿＿＿＿＿＿＿
- (전치사구) → ＿＿＿＿＿＿＿＿＿
- (동격절) → ＿＿＿＿＿＿＿＿＿
- 동사 → ＿＿＿＿＿＿＿＿＿
- 목적어 → ＿＿＿＿＿＿＿＿＿

Writing

다음 밑줄 친 우리말을 문맥에 맞게 영작하시오.

1. Americans ~을 끈질기게 요구해오고 있다 the normalization of the beef trade.

   └▸ ....

2. Defining 'normalization' 하기 쉬운 일이 아니다.

   └▸ ....

3. Scientists tell the public that by eating infected beef they 소가 지닌 같은 질병을 얻을 수 있다.

   └▸ ....

4. Citizens cannot put a burger to their lips ~을 의심하지 않고서는 if the beef patty will make them go crazy.

   └▸ ....

5. 그 이유는 ~라는 것이다 the animals' brain and central nervous system are being broken down by the disease.

   └▸ ....

The human brain is composed of more than 100 billion neurons (nerve cells) through which electric pulses travel at more 400 km an hour. The pulses generated by the electrically excitable membrane of the neuron are commands sent by the brain telling different parts of the body what to do. As these electric pulses travel throughout our body they are actually creating sufficient electricity  to power a light bulb. The production of electricity obviously requires a fuel source which in this case is the food we eat. The brain is a huge consumer of caloric energy, using up an impressive 20% of the calories we eat.

Not only is the brain's composition special, but so is its capacity. It is estimated that the mental capacity of a 100-year old human with perfect memory could be represented by a computer with 10 to the power of 15 bits (one petabit). At the current rate of computer chip development, that figure can be reached in about 35 years. (a) _____, that represents just memory capacity, not the extremely complex processes of thought creation and emotions.

It is often thought that only a few special people possess photographic memory, but this is not true. According to scientists, anyone can train his or her brain so that he or she has 'photographic memory.' Orangutans and dolphins like humans can recognize themselves in a mirror, but only humans seem to quickly forget what they look like once they turn away from a mirror. Can you draw a picture of yourself without looking in a mirror? A few people can do this by training the brain. (b) _____, our capacity to memorize is not something we are born with. We need to train our brains in order to use this capacity.

Words _____

• **neuron** [njúərɑn] 뉴런 (신경 단위)   • **excitable** [iksáitəbəl] 자극받기 쉬운   • **membrane** [mémbrein] 세포막
• **light bulb** 전구   • **use up** 다 써버리다   • **impressive** [imprésiv] 인상적인   • **figure** [fígjər] 숫자
• **photographic memory** 사진처럼 선명한 기억력

Info Scan

1. Which of the following is true about neurons? (choose two)

① They issue commands to each part of the body.
② They are cells that process and transmit information.
③ They create enough electricity to power a house.
④ They can be found in each part of human body.
⑤ They create electric pulses that travel through our body.

Inference

2. Why does the author mention thought creation and emotions in paragraph 2?

① to imply that computers can later create thoughts and emotions
② to explain why computers are often compared with human brains
③ to imply that it is impossible for computers to surpass human brains
④ to indicate what the future aims of advanced technologies are
⑤ to show what counts the most when considering brain capacity

Detail

3. 밑줄 친 10 to the power of 15 bits를 숫자로 표현하시오.

.... bits

Coherence

4. 빈칸 (a)와 (b)에 들어갈 알맞은 말로 짝지어진 것은?

	(a)		(b)
①	Besides	⋯	Furthermore
②	However	⋯	In the meantime
③	Otherwise	⋯	In addition
④	However	⋯	In other words
⑤	By the way	⋯	Moreover

 ## Grammar 〈so + 동사 + 주어〉 vs. 〈so + 주어 + 동사〉

- Not only is the brain's composition special, but so is its capacity.
- + You said it was good, and so it is.

Tips 〈so+주어+(조)동사〉는 선행의 진술에 대하여 동의·확인을 나타내어 '정말로, 참으로, 실제'라는 의미를 나타낸다. 반면 〈so+(조)동사+주어〉는 다른 주어에 딸린 긍정의 진술에 덧붙여 '…도 역시(또한)'이라는 의미이다.

▎ Quiz **다음을 영작하시오.**

1. A: 너 매우 기쁜 것 같구나. — B: 정말 그래요.
   → A: You look very happy. — B: _____ .
2. A: 지난 여름에 나는 파리에 있었다. — B: 나도 그랬어.
   → A: I was in Paris last summer. — B: _____ .

Structure 분사구의 명사 수식

The pulses generated by the electrically excitable membrane of the neuron are commands sent by the brain telling different parts of the body what to do.

◎ The pulses란 어떤 전파를 이야기하는가?
   → ....

◎ commands란 어떤 명령을 말하는가?
   → ....

문장의 구조	주어 + 동사 + 보어 + (분사구) + (분사구)

- 주어 → .... · (분사구) → ....
- 동사 → .... · (분사구) → ....
- 보어 → ....

Writing

다음 밑줄 친 우리말을 문맥에 맞게 영작하시오.

1. The human brain is composed of more than 100 billion neurons 뉴런
   을 통해서 전기펄스가 이동하는 at more 400 km an hour.

   ⌐→
   ....

2. These electric pulses are actually creating sufficient electricity 전구
   하나를 켤 수 있는.

   ⌐→
   ....

3. 두뇌의 구성이 특별할 뿐만 아니라, but so is its capacity.

   ⌐→
   ....

4. But only humans seem to quickly forget 그들이 어떻게 생겼는지를 once
   they turn away from a mirror.

   ⌐→
   ....

5. Our capacity to memorize is not 우리가 가지고 태어나는 어떤 것.

   ⌐→
   ....

Review

A 다음 단어의 뜻을 쓰시오.

01. adapt _____
02. cattle _____
03. concentrate _____
04. diplomatic _____
05. extreme _____
06. fatal _____

07. lay _____
08. skeptical _____
09. sufficient _____
10. tadpole _____
11. territory _____
12. use up _____

B A의 단어를 활용하여 다음 우리말에 맞게 영작하시오.

01. 극심한 가난 _____

02. 한 무리의 소 (herd) _____

03. 불치의 병, 죽을 병 _____

04. 돈을 다 써버리다 _____

05. 외교 관계를 수립하다 (establish) _____

06. 내 새가 알을 낳았다. _____

C A의 단어를 활용하여 다음 문장의 빈칸에 문맥상 알맞은 말을 쓰시오.

01. If you are _____ about something, you have doubts about it.

02. _____ are small water creatures that grow into frogs or toads.

03. _____ is land that is controlled by a particular country or ruler.

04. If something is _____ for a particular purpose, there is enough of it for the purpose.

05. If you _____ on something, you give all your attention to it.

06. Basically, to _____ is to make something or someone well suited to a certain purpose or circumstance.

D   다음 문장의 빈칸에 어법상 알맞은 것을 고르시오.

01. Heavy snow made it _____ for us to climb the mountain.
   ① impossibility   ② impossibly   ③ impossible

02. These two substances taste _____ to some people.
   ① bittered   ② bitterly   ③ bitter

03. _____ removed from the site after the announcement.
   ① A cattle was   ② Cattle were   ③ Cattles were

04. He had to _____ down on the couch for fifteen minutes before
   the meeting.
   ① lie   ② lay   ③ be lying

05. I saw the whole city _____ when the game started.
   ① emptily   ② empty   ③ emptied

06. What is your favorite item of _____ ?
   ① clothing   ② clothings   ③ a clothing

07. He _____ his clothes on his chair for the next day.
   ① lay   ② laid   ③ lied

08. The origin of the pyramid remained _____ .
   ① mystery   ② mysterious   ③ mysteriously

09. This article offers 10 tips on how to avoid mistakes while _____
   new tile in your bathroom.
   ① lying   ② laying   ③ lain

10. The proposal made by the committee sounded _____ to me.
   ① unreason   ② unreasonably   ③ unreasonable

Level
3-A

AIM HIGH 에임하이

상위권을 위한 필독서

READING 리딩

Answer Keys

In-Depth Lab

AIM HIGH 에임하이
READING 리딩

Answer Keys

We're
위아북스

Chapter 01

Vocabulary Pre-check

- abandon 포기하다
- activation 활성(화)
- adopt 채택하다
- aerospace 우주 공간
- alter 바꾸다, 변경하다
- approximately 대략
- barrier 울타리, 장벽
- byproduct 부산물
- charged 전하를 띤, 대전(帶電)한
- churn out 대량으로 발생하다
- coalesce 응집시키다
- composition 구성, 성분
- concentration 농도, 집중
- conclusively 확실하게
- consequence 결과, 영향
- consequently 그 결과
- counteract 반작용하다, (효과 등을) 없애다
- depend on ~에 달려 있다, ~에 의존하다
- determiner 결정인자
- disperse 흩뜨리다, 분산시키다
- enormous 막대한, 거대한
- eruption 분출, 폭발
- exception 예외, 제외
- exploration 탐사, 탐험
- formation 형성
- fossil 화석
- gene 유전자
- grassland 목초지
- hiccup 딸꾹질, 약간의 문제
- hypothesize 가설을 세우다
- hypothetically 가정하여
- identical 동일한
- ignition 점화
- inhabit 살다, 거주하다
- interfere with ~을 방해하다
- inversion 반대, 역적
- launch 발사하다
- master 숙달하다, 정통하다
- minute 미세한, 사소한
- moisture 수분, 습기
- navigation 항해술, 항공술
- numerous 다수의, 수많은
- obstacle 장애(물)
- opportunity 기회
- particle 미립자, 분자
- pigment 색소
- preserve 보존하다
- property 특성, 성질
- radiation 복사 에너지
- reflect 반사하다
- reflective 반사하는, 반사적인
- release 방출하다
- reveal 밝혀내다
- satellite 위성
- sequence 배열, 순서
- shed (빛을) 퍼뜨리다
- skull 두개골
- spacecraft 우주선
- specifically 명확히, 정확하게
- specimen 표본, 견본
- stock 혈통, 가계
- telecommunication 원거리통신
- the number of ~의 수
- variable 변수

| 정답 |

1. ② / ④
2. a huge amount of charged particles (solar wind) / blocks the charged particles / the Earth's magnetic field
3. • 코로나: 왜 태양의 표면보다 코로나(태양의 대기)가 더 뜨거운가
   • 태양풍: 왜 태양풍이 지구의 자기장을 뚫고 들어오는가
4. ③

| 해설 |

1. ② Most of the Sun's surface is much hotter than its atmosphere.(태양의 표면 대부분은 태양의 대기보다 훨씬 더 뜨겁다.)는 틀린 내용이다. 그 반대가 옳다. 그리고 ④ The Hinode brought some data that can explain the corona problem.(Hinode는 코로나 문제를 설명할 수 있는 데이터를 가져왔다.)에 대한 언급은 나와 있지 않다. 미션에 대한 내용이 있을 뿐이지, 그 결과에 대한 설명은 없다.
   이 글에 따르면, 다음 중 사실이 아닌 것은? (2개)
   ① 태양 플라스마 대기의 온도는 백만 켈빈을 넘는다.
   ③ 코로나 문제에 대한 명확한 설명은 되어 있지 않다.
   ⑤ 어떤 사람들은 태양의 자기 파동이 대기를 뜨겁게 한다고 믿는다.

2. 세 번째 단락을 요약하면 다음과 같을 것이다.
   → The Sun emits a huge amount of charged particles (solar wind). Usually, the Earth's magnetic field blocks the charged particles. But, sometimes, the solar wind passes through the Earth's magnetic field. (태양은 거대한 양의 전하를 띤 미립자(태양풍)를 방출한다. 일반적으로, 지구의 자기장은 그 전하를 띤 미립자를 차단한다. 하지만 때때로 태양풍은 지구의 자기장을 뚫고 지나온다.)

3. The Hinode space mission's goal is to shed light on the mysterious properties of the Sun.에서 보면, Hinode space mission이 태양의 특성에 관해 풀리지 않는 부분을 해명하는 것임을 알 수 있다. 구체적인 예로, 코로나와 태양풍에 관한 풀리지 않는 의문들이 언급되었는데, 코로나(태양 대기)가 태양 표면보다 더 뜨거운 이유

와 태양풍이 지구의 자기장을 뚫고 통신 장애를 일으키는 이유에 대한 연구가 있을 것이라는 내용이다.

4. 마지막 단락에서 보면, 태양에 관해 풀리지 않는 부분들에 대한 가설들이 있다는 것을 알 수 있다. 즉 정답은 ③ There are some theories regarding unknown facts about the Sun.(태양에 대해 알려지지 않은 사실에 관한 몇 가지 이론들이 있다.)이다.
   다음 중 이 글에서 추론할 수 있는 것은?
   ① 태양을 연구하는 다른 우주선들도 있다.
   ② Hinode는 일본 사람들에 의해 발사된 첫 번째 우주선이다.
   ④ Hinode 미션은 충분한 정보를 발견할 때까지 계속될 것이다.
   ⑤ 과학자들은 태양 연구를 위해 또 다른 발사를 계획하고 있다.

| 본문 |

Launched in September 2006, the Hinode spacecraft has been orbiting the Earth so as to keep a constant view of the Sun. The Hinode space mission's goal — "Hinode" is Japanese for "sunrise" — is to shed light on the mysterious properties of the Sun. The mission is led by the Japan Aerospace Exploration Agency, with cooperation from several other space agencies.

First of all, the Hinode mission hopes to aid scientists in understanding the "corona problem," that the Sun's corona is much hotter than the visible surface of the Sun. The temperature on the Sun's surface is incredibly hot, about 6,000 Kelvin (water boils at 373 Kelvin on Earth), but not so hot when compared to the Sun's plasma atmosphere, or corona, which is estimated to be one to three million Kelvin. Scientists have not been able to conclusively explain the reason for this temperature inversion. One theory relates to the discovery of magnetic waves which pass through the plasma of the Sun's corona. It is thought that these waves might be releasing energy which is heating the corona.

Secondly, scientists hope the Hinode mission will help them understand why solar wind generated by the Sun sometimes interferes with telecommunications, navigation and electrical power systems on Earth. Solar wind is the huge amount of charged particles that the Sun churns out into space. The Earth's magnetic field usually creates a barrier which protects the Earth from these charged particles, but not always. Scientists want to know why this magnetic barrier is not full-proof. They hypothesize that magnetic energy eruptions on the Sun may interfere with the Earth's magnetic barrier, but they really aren't sure.

| 해석 |

2006년 9월에 발사된, Hinode 우주선은 태양을 계속 지켜보기 위해 지구의 궤도를 돌고 있다. Hinode 우주 미션 목적 — Hinode란 "일출"이라는 일본어이다 — 은 태양의 신비스러운 특성을 밝혀내는 것이다. 그 미션은 몇몇 다른 우주기관들의 협조를 얻어 일본 우주 탐사 기관에 의해 진행되고 있다.

무엇보다도, Hinode 미션은 과학자들로 하여금 태양의 코로나가 태양의 눈에 보이는 표면보다 훨씬 더 뜨겁다는 "코로나 문제"를 이해하는 데 도움을 주고자 하는 것이다. 태양 표면의 온도는 약 6,000켈빈(물은 지구에서 373켈빈에서 끊는다)으로 믿을 수 없을 만큼 뜨겁지만, 태양의 플라스마 대기, 즉 코로나와 비교할 때 그렇게 뜨거운 것이 아닌데, 코로나는 1~3백만 켈빈이라고 추정된다. 과학자들은 이 온도 역전에 대한 이유를 확실하게 설명하지 못했다. 한 이론은 태양 코로나의 플라스마를 통해 흐르는 자기 파동의 발견과 관련이 있다. 이 파장들이 코로나를 뜨겁게 하는 에너지를 방출하고 있을지 모른다고 생각된다.

둘째로, 과학자들은 Hinode 미션이 태양에 의해 생성되는 태양풍이 때때로 왜 지구의 원거리통신, 네비게이션과 전력 시스템을 방해하는지 이해하는 데 도움이 되길 바라고 있다. 태양풍은 태양이 우주로 대량 방출하는 거대한 양의 전하를 띤 미립자이다. 일반적으로 지구의 자기장은 이 전하를 띤 미립자들로부터 지구를 보호하는 방벽을 만드는데, 항상 그렇지는 않다. 과학자들은 이 자기장 방벽이 완전히 막아내지 못하는 이유를 알고 싶어한다. 그들은 태양에서의 자기에너지 분출이 지구의 자기 방벽을 간섭한다는 가설을 세웠지만, 정말로 확신하는 것은 아니다.

| 구문 |

• Launched in September 2006, the Hinode spacecraft has been orbiting the Earth

Launched in September 2006는 분사구문으로, 그 앞에 Being이 생략되었다고 볼 수 있다.

• the "corona problem," that the Sun's corona is much hotter than the visible surface of the Sun

that 이하는 the "corona problem"과 동격이며, 비교급을 강조할 때는 much, even, far, still, a lot 등을 쓸 수 있다.

GRAMMAR Quiz

1. 당신이 비난을 전적으로 면할 수는 있는 것은 아니다.
   → You're not entirely free from blame.

2. 모든 책이 재미를 주거나 이득을 주는 것은 아니다.
   → Not all books interest or profit us.

3. 인생에서 성공은 부의 획득과 반드시 동일한 것은 아니다.
   → Success in life is not necessarily the same thing as the acquirement of riches.

STRUCTURE

The temperature on the Sun's surface is incredibly hot, about 6,000 Kelvin, but not so hot when compared to the Sun's plasma atmosphere, or corona, which is estimated to be one to three million Kelvin.

❍ not so hot 앞에 생략되었을 말은?
   → the temperature on the Sun's surface is

❍ when과 compared 사이에 생략되었을 말은?
   → the temperature on the Sun's surface is

〈문장의 구조〉

• 주어   → The temperature on the Sun's surface
• 동사   → is
• 보어   → incredibly hot, about 6,000 Kelvin
• 연결어   → but
• 보어   → not so hot
• (부사절) → when compared to the Sun's plasma atmosphere, or corona
• (관계사절) → which is estimated to be one to three million Kelvin

1. The Hinode spacecraft has been orbiting the Earth so as to keep a constant view of the Sun.
   (~을 계속 지켜보기 위해)

2. The Sun's corona is much hotter than the visible surface of the Sun. (~보다 훨씬 더 뜨겁다)

3. The temperature on the Sun's surface is not so hot when compared to the Sun's plasma atmosphere, or corona. (~와 비교할 때)

4. It is thought that these waves might be releasing energy which is heating the corona.
   (~라고 생각된다)

5. Scientists want to know why this magnetic barrier is not full-proof.
   (이 자기장 방벽이 완전히 막아내지 못하는 이유)

Passage 02

| 정답 |

1. ①
2. • 결과: 네안데르탈인과 현대인의 MC1R 배열이 다르지만, 멜라닌 생성에 미치는 영향은 같다.
   • 결론: 빨간 머리와 하얀 피부를 가진 네안데르탈인들이 존재했을 것이다.
3. ②
4. ②

| 해설 |

1. Since the actual hair and skin of Neanderthals have not been preserved라는 내용으로 보아, 네안데르탈인의의 머리카락과 피부는 보존되어 있지 않다는 것을 알 수 있다, 그러므로 ① Scientists have studied the hair and skin attached to Neanderthal fossils.(과학자들은 네안데르탈인의 화석에 붙어 있는 머리카락과 피부를 연구해왔다.)가 옳지 않다.
   이 글에 따르면, 다음 중 옳지 않은 것은?
   ② MC1R 유전자 배열이 인간에게 있어 머리카락과 피부색을 결정하는 것이다.

③ 현대 인간의 MC1R 배열은 네안데르탈인의 그것과 다르다.

④ 인간에게 있어 세포로 하여금 멜라닌을 생성하도록 지시하는 것은 MC1R 유전자이다.

⑤ 네안데르탈인의 발견된 화석이 정보의 유일한 자료였다.

2. 실험 결과, 네안데르탈인의 MC1R 유전자는 현대 인간의 MC1R 유전자와는 그 배열이 다르기는 하지만, 빨간 머리카락과 하얀 피부의 결정 요인인 멜라닌 생성에 미치는 영향은 현대 인간의 그것과 같고, 그래서 결론은 빨간 머리와 하얀 피부를 가진 네안데르탈인들이 존재했을 것이라는 것이다.

3. identical은 「아주 동일한, 일치하는」이라는 뜻이므로 같은 의미의 단어는 ② alike이다.
   ① 식별할 수 있는   ③ 다른
   ④ 분리된   ⑤ 구별되는

4. 주어진 문장의 The researchers로 보아 연구진에 대한 설명이 나온 후에 들어가야 한다는 것을 알 수 있다. 또한 DNA samples를 분석한 후, MC1R 유전자 배열을 정확하게 조사하게 되는 순서가 적절하므로, 주어진 문장은 (B)에 들어가야 한다.

| 본문 |

Have you ever seen a picture of a Neanderthal caveman with red hair and pale skin? Probably not. But a European research team has found that hypothetically speaking some Neanderthals who inhabited Europe and Central Asia approximately 230,000 to 30,000 years ago could have had such hair color as well as light skin. Since the actual hair and skin of Neanderthals have not been preserved, all the knowledge we have of Neanderthals comes from examining fossils such as skull bones.

Carles Lalueza, a professor of the University of Barcelona, and some assistant researchers studied DNA samples from Neanderthal fossils. The researchers analyzed DNA samples from two Neanderthal specimens from Spain and Italy. They looked specifically at the sequence of the MC1R gene. In modern humans of European stock, this gene is responsible for pale skin and red hair since this DNA sequence directs cells to produce the pigment melanin which is the primary determiner of hair and skin color in humans.

The research, however, revealed that this gene and the one in modern humans are not <u>identical</u>. Wanting to find out how this Neanderthal gene affected melanin production, they conducted further tests. They inserted the Neanderthal gene into cells that were growing in a test tube. The results showed that even though the Neanderthal MC1R gene and the modern human MC1R gene were different, they had the same effect on the production of melanin. Consequently, the researchers conclude that it is possible that there were red-haired and fair-skinned Neanderthals.

| 해석 |

빨간 머리에 하얀 피부를 가진 네안데르탈 동굴인의 사진을 본 적이 있는가? 아마도 없을 것이다. 그러나 유럽의 연구팀은 가정하여 말하면 대략 23만 년 전부터 3만 년 전까지 유럽과 중앙아시아에 살았던 어떤 네안데르탈인들은 투명한 피부뿐만 아니라 그런 머리색을 가지고 있었을 수도 있다는 것을 알아냈다. 네안데르탈인의 실제 머리와 피부가 보존되어 있지 않기 때문에, 우리가 네안데르탈인에 대해 가지고 있는 모든 지식은 두개골 뼈와 같은 화석을 조사한 것에서 나온다.

바르셀로나 대학의 교수인 Carles Lalueza와 몇몇 조교 연구원들은 네안데르탈인의 화석에서 나온 DNA 샘플을 연구했다. 그 연구진은 스페인과 이탈리아에서 나온 두 개의 네안데르탈인 표본에서 DNA 샘플을 분석했다. 그들은 MC1R 유전자 배열을 정확하게 조사했다. 유럽 혈통의 현대 인류에서, 이 유전자는 하얀 피부와 빨간 머리의 원인인데, 왜냐하면 이 DNA 배열이 세포로 하여금 인간의 머리카락과 피부색의 주요 결정인자인 멜라닌 색소를 생성하라고 지시하기 때문이다.

그러나 그 연구는 이 유전자와 현대 인류의 그것이 동일하지 않다는 것을 밝혀냈다. 네안데르탈인의 이 유전자가 멜라닌 생성에 어떻게 영향을 미치는지 발견하고자, 그들은 실험을 더 했다. 그들은 네안데르탈인의 유전자를 실험용 튜브에서 자라나고 있던 세포에 주입했다. 결과는 네안데르탈인의 MC1R 유전자와 현대 인간의 MC1R 유전자가 다른데도 불구하고, 멜라닌 생성에 대해서는 같은 효과를 가지고 있다는

것을 보여 주었다. 따라서 그 연구진은 빨간 머리카락에 하얀 피부의 네안데르탈인들이 존재했을 가능성이 있다고 결론 내렸다.

| 구문 |

• Have you ever seen a picture of a Neanderthal caveman with red hair and pale skin?
현재완료 〈have+p.p.〉는 ever와 함께 쓰여 경험을 나타낸다.

• Wanting to find out how this Neanderthal gene affected melanin production, they conducted further tests.
Wanting ~ production까지는 분사구문이다. find out의 목적어로 how 의문명사절이 왔다.

GRAMMAR Quiz

1. She is not a musician but writes novels.
   → She is not a musician but a novelist.

2. I would like both free time and to be given extra money.
   → I would like both free time and extra money.

3. We found the hotel very convenient and was not too expensive.
   → We found the hotel very convenient and not too expensive.

STRUCTURE

Some Neanderthals who inhabited Europe and Central Asia approximately 230,000 to 30,000 years ago could have had such hair color as well as light skin.

❍ Some Neanderthals란 어떤 사람들인가?
   → who inhabited Europe and ~ 30,000 years ago

〈문장의 구조〉
• 주어 → Some Neanderthals who inhabited Europe and ~ 30,000 years ago
• 동사 → could have had
• 목적어 → such hair color as well as light skin

WRITING

1. But a European research team has found that hypothetically speaking some Neanderthals could have had such hair color as well as light skin. (그런 머리색을 가지고 있었을 수도 있다)

2. All the knowledge we have of Neanderthals comes from examining fossils such as skull bones. (화석을 조사한 것에서 나온다)

3. This DNA sequence directs cells to produce the pigment melanin which is the primary determiner of hair and skin color in humans. (세포로 하여금 ~을 생성하라고 지시하다)

4. The research, however, revealed that this gene and the one in modern humans are not identical. (동일하지 않다)

5. The researchers conclude that it is possible that there were red-haired and fair-skinned Neanderthals. (빨간 머리카락에 하얀 피부의 네안데르탈인들)

03
Passage

| 정답 |

1. ④
2. • 영향 1: 태양빛을 더 잘 반사한다.
   • 영향 2: 더 오랫동안 구름인 상태를 유지한다.
3. 지구 온난화를 방지할 수 있을 거라는 기대 때문에
4. ⑤

| 해설 |

1. Aerosols are a natural byproduct of chemical processes occurring in volcanoes, dust storms, sea spray, grassland fires and a host of other natural activities.라는 문장에서 ④ Aerosols can be created from many different Earth activities.(에어로졸은 많은 다른 지구 활동들에서 생겨날 수 있다.)의 내용을 확인할 수 있다.

   주어진 글에 의하면, 다음 중 사실인 것은?

① 에어로졸은 자연에서와 비슷한 인간 활동을 초래한다.
② 에어로졸은 지구 온난화의 주요 요인 중 하나이다.
③ 에어로졸은 해로운 태양빛 대부분을 우주로 다시 반사한다.
⑤ 에어로졸은 위험한 수준까지 지구의 온도를 낮출 수 있다.

2. 에어로졸은 구름의 씨앗이 될 수 있고, 두 가지 영향을 미칠 수 있다. 그 영향은 This has two consequences — clouds with smaller drops reflect more sunlight, and such clouds last longer라는 문장에서 알 수 있다. 즉, 빛을 더 잘 반사하고 더 오랫동안 구름인 상태를 유지하게 하는 것이다.

3. 과학자들이 aerosols에 관심을 갖는 이유는 Scientists are wondering if the cooling effect of aerosols will counteract the greenhouse effect which has been warming the Earth's surface for the last few decades.에서 알 수 있다. 즉, 지구 온난화를 방지할 수 있을지도 모른다는 기대 때문이다.

4. 주어진 문장의 Both the effects는 마지막 문장의 This has two consequences의 내용이다. 즉 그 문장이 끝나는 (E)에 들어가는 것이 가장 적절하다.

| 본문 |

Aerosols, which are minute particles in the air, are produced naturally and by human actions. Aerosols are a natural byproduct of chemical processes occurring in volcanoes, dust storms, sea spray, grassland fires and a host of other natural activities. Numerous human actions which can be in fact copies of natural actions thus also create aerosols.

Aerosols have the effect of cooling the Earth's surface since they reflect light from the sun back into space. When this occurs, less solar radiation warms the Earth's surface. The degree to which the Earth is cooled depends on many variables, such as the size and composition of the particles, as well as the reflective properties of the materials on the Earth's surface immediately below the aerosols. Scientists are wondering if the cooling effect of aerosols will counteract the greenhouse effect which has been warming the Earth's surface for the last few decades.

Aerosols are also thought to indirectly influence the climate of the Earth by altering the composition of clouds. In fact, without aerosols in the atmosphere, there would be no clouds. Minute aerosol particles are the "seeds" which begin the process of the formation of cloud droplets. As the number of aerosol particles increases inside a cloud, the moisture in that cloud disperses into each aerosol particle thus reducing the concentration of water in each particle. This has two consequences — clouds with smaller drops reflect more sunlight, and such clouds last longer, because it takes more time for small drops to coalesce into drops that are large enough to fall to the ground. Both the effects increase the amount of sunlight that is reflected into space without reaching the surface.

| 해석 |

에어로졸, 그것은 공기 중에 있는 미립자인데, 자연적으로 그리고 인간의 행위로 생겨난다. 에어로졸은 화산, 먼지 폭풍, 바다 물안개, 목초지의 화재와 많은 다른 자연 활동 중에 일어나는 화학 작용의 자연적인 부산물이다. 따라서, 사실상 자연 활동의 모방이라 할 수 있는 수많은 인간 활동 또한 이 에어로졸을 만들어내게 되는 것이다.

에어로졸은 태양으로부터 오는 빛을 우주로 다시 반사하기 때문에 지구를 냉각시키는 효과를 지니고 있다. 이런 일이 일어나면, 더 적은 태양 에너지가 지구의 표면을 덥힌다. 지구가 시원해질 수 있는 온도는 에어로졸 바로 아래 지구 표면에 있는 물질이 지닌 반사의 성질뿐만 아니라, 에어로졸 분자의 크기나 구성 같은 여러 가지 변수에 따라 다르다. 과학자들은 에어로졸의 냉각효과가 지난 몇 십 년 동안 지구 표면을 덥혀 오고 있는 온실효과를 없애 주지 않을까 생각하고 있다.

에어로졸은 또한 구름의 성분을 바꿈으로써, 지구의 기후에 간접적으로 영향을 미친다고 여겨진다. 사실, 대기 중에 에어로졸이 없다면, 구름도 없을 것이다. 미세한 에어로졸 분자가 구름 방울 형성 과정을 시작하는 "씨앗"인 것이다. 구름 안에 에어로졸 분자의 수가 증가함에 따라, 그 구름 속에 있는 수분이 각각의 에어로졸 분자로 흩어지고 따라서 각 분자 안에 있는 수분의 농도를 줄어들게 한다. 이것은 두 가지 결과를 낳는다 — 더 적은 물방울들을 가진 구름은 더 많은 태양빛을 반사하고, 그러한 구름들은 더 오랫동안 지속되는데, 왜냐하면 적은 물방울들이 땅으로 떨어질 만큼 충분히 많은 물방울로 응집되는 데에는 더 많은 시간이 걸리기 때문이다. 두 가지 효과 모두 지구 표면에 도달하지 않고 우주로 반사되는 태양빛의 양을 증가시킨다.

| 구문 |

- Aerosols, which are minute particles in the air, are produced naturally and by human actions.
  콤마 뒤의 which는 Aerosols를 선행사로 하는 관계대명사 계속적 용법이며, Aerosols를 부연설명하고 있다.

- the greenhouse effect which has been warming the Earth's surface for the last few decades
  which는 주격 관계대명사로, the greenhouse effect를 선행사로 하고 있다. has been warming은 예전부터 지금까지 계속적으로 진행 중이라는 것을 표현하는 현재완료진행형이다.

- it takes more time for small drops to coalesce into drops
  〈it takes＋시간＋(for＋주체)＋to부정사〉는 'for 이하가 to 부정사하는 데 얼마의 시간이 걸리다' 라는 것을 표현한다.

GRAMMAR Quiz

1. 중력이 없다면, 사과는 땅에 떨어지지 않을 것이다.
   → Without gravity, an apple would not fall to the ground.

2. 그 기술이 아니었다면, 그 학습경험이 유용할 수 있을까?
   → Would the learning experience be available but for the technology?

STRUCTURE

The degree to which the Earth is cooled depends on many variables, such as the size and composition of the particles, as well as the reflective properties of the materials on the Earth's surface immediately below the aerosols.

◉ The degree란 어떤 온도를 말하는가?
   → to which the Earth is cooled
   → 해석: 지구가 시원해질 수 있는 온도

◉ many variables란 어떤 변수들을 말하는지 두 가지 쓰시오.
   → the size and composition of the participles
   → the reflective properties ~ below the aerosols

〈문장의 구조〉

• 주어 → The degree to which the Earth is cooled
• 동사 → depends on
• 목적어 → many variables
• (부사구) → such as the size and composition of the participles
• (부사구) → as well as the reflective properties of the materials
• (부사구) → on the Earth's surface
• (부사구) → immediately below the aerosols

WRITING

1. Aerosols have the effect of cooling the Earth's surface. (~하는 효과를 지니고 있다)

2. The degree depends on many variables, such as the size and composition of the particles, as well as the reflective properties.
(여러 가지 변수에 따라 다르다)

3. The cooling effect of aerosols will counteract the greenhouse effect which has been warming the Earth's surface for the last few decades.
(~을 덮혀 오고 있는)

4. In fact, without aerosols in the atmosphere, there would be no clouds.
(구름도 없을 것이다)

5. It takes more time for small drops to coalesce into drops that are large enough to fall to the ground. ((~가 …하는 데에) 더 많은 시간이 걸리다)

Passage 04

| 정답 |

1. ⑤
2. the flight operation system that they had been working with
3. 운영 시스템의 문제점 발견으로 인한 새로운 운영 시스템으로 교체 / 로켓 엔진의 문제 발견으로 인해 엔진 수리 또는 교체
4. three times

| 해석 |

1. 두 번째 단락을 보면, 발사 팀은 새로운 운영 시스템에 대해 숙달해야 했고, 게다가 또 다른 문제가 생겨서 새로운 것으로 교체해야 했다. 여기서 ⑤ It took several months for the team to learn about the new operation system.(발사 팀이 새로운 운영 시스템에 대해 배우는 데 수개월이 걸렸다.)의 내용을 알 수 있다.
다음 중 내용이 일치하는 것은?
① 테라 프로젝트 매니저는 위성을 발사해 본 경험이 그리 많지 않았다.
② 테라 위성을 발사대에 장착하는 데 48시간이 걸렸다.
③ 발사 팀은 거의 1년 동안 이전의 운영 시스템을 수리해야 했다.
④ 첫 번째 발사 시도는 로켓 엔진 중 하나 때문에 실패했다.

2. 밑줄 친 it이 가리키는 말은 바로 앞에 나와 있는 the flight operation system that they had been working with이다.

3. Terra 발사가 지연된 첫 번째 이유는 비행 운영 시스템의 문제점이었고, 두 번째 장애물은 로켓 엔진의 문제였다.

4. 첫 번째와 두 번째의 장애는 직접적으로 드러나 있으며, 세 번째 지연은 마지막 48시간 동안 더 완전한 준비를 위한 것이었으므로, 세 번 연기되었다는 것을 알 수 있다.
테라 발사는 몇 번 연기되었는가? (영어로)

| 본문 |

Before the "ignition button" is pushed to launch a satellite, an enormous number of obstacles have usually been overcome. Projects of this nature normally have tons of hiccups along the way and Terra, launched on December 18, 1999, was no exception to this rule. Terra Project Manager Kevin Grady is a positive manager who sees the glass as half full rather than half empty. And he needed to overcome the obstacles in the project's way.

The first obstacle was that Grady's veteran launch team had to master a new flight operation system that had never before been used by NASA. Six months before the initial launch date in December 1998, mission managers realized that the flight operation system that they had been working with had too many problems and they decided to abandon it and adopt a new one. Consequently, the launch date was delayed for six months.

Then close to the launch date a company supplying rockets that would be used to launch Terra into space discovered that the rocket's engine had a serious problem which could cause a launch failure. Since they had to fix or replace it with a new one, a new launch date had to be set, again!

As the new date of December 16 approached, Grady kept his team thinking positively, telling them "Spacecraft operations and activation provide opportunities for us to excel." On the 16th, Grady thought his team was "well prepared" and there would be no further delays. Even though Grady and his team were well prepared, Terra stood ready on the launch pad another 48 hours before lift off.

| 해석 |

위성을 발사하기 위해 "점화 버튼"을 누르기 전에, 보통 수많은 장애들이 극복되기 마련이다. 일반적으로 이런 성질의 프로젝트가 진행되는 과정엔 많은 문제들이 있기 마련이고, 1999년 12월 18일에 발사된 테라도 예외가 아니었다. 테라 프로젝트 매니저 Kevin Grady는 유리잔이 절반 비었다기보다는 절반 채워져 있다고 보는 긍정적인 사람이다. 그리고 그는 그 프로젝트가 진행되는 동안 문제점을 극복해내야 했다.

첫 번째 장애물은 Grady의 숙련된 발사팀이 NASA에 의해 전혀 사용되어 본 적이 없던 새로운 비행 운영 시스템을 숙달해야만 했다는 것이다. 1998년 12월 초기 발사 날짜 6개월 전에, 미션 매니저들은 그들이 일해오고 있던 그 비행 운영 시스템에 너무 많은 문제가 있다는 것을 알게 되었고, 그래서 그것을 포기하고 새로운 것을 채택하기로 결정했다. 그 결과, 발사일은 6개월 뒤로 미뤄졌다.

그리고 나서 발사일이 가까워졌을 때, 테라를 우주에 발사시키는 데 사용될 로켓을 공급하는 회사가 그 로켓의 엔진에 발사를 실패하게 할 수 있는 심각한 문제가 있다는 것을 알아냈다. 그래서 그들은 그것을 수리하거나 새로운 것으로 교체해야 했고, 또 다시 새로운 발사일을 정해야 했다!

새로운 날짜인 12월 16일이 다가오자, Grady는 그의 팀이 긍정적으로 생각하게끔 했고, 그들에게 "우주선 계획과 활성화는 우리가 도약할 기회를 제공합니다."라고 말했다. 16일에 Grady는 그의 팀이 "잘 준비되었다"고 생각해서 더 이상의 지연은 없을 것이라고 생각했다. Grady와 그의 팀이 아주 잘 준비되어 있었음에도 불구하고, 테라는 이륙하기 전에 48시간을 더 발사대에서 대기하고 있어야 했다.

| 구문 |

- a positive manager who sees the glass as half full rather than half empty / a new flight operation system that had never before been used by NASA / a serious problem which could cause a launch failure

who, that, which는 모두 주격 관계대명사로 생략할 수 없다는 점에 유의한다.

- the flight operation system that they had been working with had too many problems

that은 with의 목적어 the flight operation을 선행사로 하며 목적격 관계대명사로 생략할 수 있다. 즉, the flight operation system they had been working with had too many problems로 쓰일 수 있다. 또한 전치사 with를 관계대명사 앞으로 보내면, that 대신 which를 써서 the flight operation system with which they had been working had too many problems가 된다.

GRAMMAR Quiz

1. 너는 노트북 컴퓨터가 있니? — 아니, 하지만 우리 오빠는 하나 있어. 그는 그것을 어제 샀거든.

→ Do you have a notebook computer? — No,

but my brother has one. He bought it
yesterday.

2. 미국의 수도는 일본의 수도보다 더 크다.
  → The capital of the U.S.A. is larger than that of
    Japan.

STRUCTURE

The flight operation system that they had been
working with had too many problems.

◐ The flight operation system은 어떤 운영 시스템을
말하는가?
  → that they had been working with
  → 해석: 그들이 일해오고 있던 비행 운영 시스템

〈문장의 구조〉
• 주어 → The flight operation system that they
            had been working with
• 동사 → had
• 목적어 → too many problems

WRITING

1. Terra, launched on December 18, 1999, <u>was no
   exception to this rule.</u> (이 규칙에 예외가 아니었다)

2. Terra Project Manager Kevin Grady is a positive
   manager who sees the glass as half full <u>rather
   than half empty.</u> (절반 비었다기보다는)

3. The first obstacle was that Grady's veteran
   launch team had to master a new flight
   operation system that <u>had never before been
   used</u> by NASA. (전혀 사용되어 본 적이 없었다)

4. A company supplying rockets <u>that would be
   used to launch</u> Terra into space discovered that
   the rocket's engine had a serious problem.
   (~을 발사시키는 데 사용될)

5. Grady thought his team was "well prepared"
   and <u>there would be no further delays.</u>
   (더 이상의 지연은 없을 것이다)

Review

| A |

01. 채택하다
02. 응집시키다
03. 분출, 폭발
04. 화석
05. 가설을 세우다
06. ~에 살다, ~에 거주하다
07. ~을 방해하다, 간섭하다
08. 미세한, 사소한
09. 장애(물)
10. 보존하다
11. 위성
12. 배열, 순서

| B |

01. minute differences
02. eruption of a volcano
03. preserved food
04. inhabit a forest
05. obstacles to success
06. interfere with cultural development

| C |

01. fossil
02. coalesce
03. adopt
04. hypothesize
05. satellite
06. sequence

| D |

01. ①
02. ②
03. ③
04. ③
05. ①
06. ②
07. ②
08. ③
09. ③
10. ①

Chapter 02

Vocabulary Pre-check

- abruptly 갑작스럽게
- adhere to ~에 집착하다, 고수하다
- alter 변경하다, 바꾸다
- aqueduct 수로, 도수관
- artificial 인공의
- association 협회, 단체
- astronomer 천문학자
- attain 획득하다, 얻다
- be concerned about ~에 관심이 있다
- be familiar with ~을 잘 알고 있다
- be released from ~에 벗어나다
- canal 운하
- civil engineer 토목 기사
- colossal 거대한, 굉장한
- consumption 소비
- contrary to ~와는 달리
- critical 꼭 필요한
- curl 감다, 비틀다
- curve 구부리다
- despicable 야비한, 비열한
- devotee 열성가
- discard 버리다
- distribution 보급, 배분
- diversity 다양성, 변화
- dose (약의) 1회분
- ensure 확실하게 하다
- eruption 분출
- feasible 편리한, 용이한
- feat 묘기, 재주, 곡예
- feed 먹이를 먹이다
- flap (날개를) 펄럭이다
- flatten 평평하게 하다
- flexible 유연한, 구부리기 쉬운
- fountain 샘
- genetically 유전적으로
- gradient 경사도, 기울기
- gymnastics 체육
- hygiene 위생 상태, 청결함

- immense 막대한
- impose 부과하다
- imprison 구속하다, 감금하다
- incredible 믿을 수 없는, 엄청난
- ingredient 성분, 재료
- intricate 복잡한, 뒤얽힌
- mass produce 대량 생산하다
- mimic 흉내내다, 모방하다
- molecule 분자
- no longer 더 이상 ~가 아니다
- nourishment 음식물, 영양
- pass on to ~에게 물려주다
- pill 알약
- predict 예측하다
- preservation 보호, 보존
- protein 단백질
- purity 순수, 청결
- reform 개혁
- reincarnation 환생
- release 해방
- reliable 확실한, 믿을 수 있는
- removal 제거
- resident 거주자
- reveal 드러내다
- rigid 엄격한
- sect 학파
- sewage 하수 오물
- sophisticated 복잡한
- subject 과목, 주제
- suck 빨다, 빨아 먹다
- tablet 정제
- territory 영토
- tyrant 폭군
- uncertainty 불확실성

| 정답 |

1. ④
2. 날면서 날개를 구부리거나 비틀면서 끊임없이 방향을 바꾼다.
3. ⑤
4. ④

| 해설 |

1. The intricate nature of the bats' flight patterns shocked scientists at first because they were so much different than the flight patterns of birds which scientists thought would be similar to bats. 에서 보면 박쥐의 비행 패턴과 새들의 비행 패턴이 많이 다르다는 것을 알 수 있다. 그러므로 ④ Bats' flight patterns are very similar to those of many birds.(박쥐의 비행 패턴은 많은 새들의 그것과 매우 비슷하다.)가 틀리다.   글의 내용에 따라 다음 중 사실이 아닌 것은?
   ① 어떤 박쥐들은 사물을 보기 위해서 눈에 의존한다.
   ② 어떤 박쥐들은 날아다니기 위해 음파에 의존한다.
   ③ 어떤 박쥐들은 야채를 먹는 반면, 다른 것들은 동물의 피를 먹는다.
   ⑤ 과학자들은 박쥐처럼 날 수 있는 장치를 만들려고 노력하고 있다.

2. Rather the wings of bats curve, curl, and change direction constantly as they fly.에서 보면 박쥐 비행의 특징은 날면서 날개를 구부리거나 비틀거나 하며 끊임없이 방향을 바꾼다는 것이다.

3. 주어진 문장의 That is because ~로 보아, 어떤 내용에 대한 원인이 된다는 것을 알 수 있다. 그러므로 현재 비행기가 박쥐처럼 날 수 없다는 내용 뒤인 (E)가 가장 적절하다.

4. 여기서 feats는 「묘기, 재주, 곡예」라는 의미이다. 같은 뜻의 어휘는 ④ stunts이다.

| 본문 |

The bat world is full of diversity. Not only do different types of bats have different diets, ranging from fruits to insects, but also some bats use sound waves to move around while others use eyes. Moreover, of the over 1,200 species of bats in the world, only a few suck blood for nourishment. But what all bats have in common is, other than being the only flying mammals in existence, flexible wings that allow them to perform flying feats. Bats change direction very quickly, turning up, down or around abruptly and unexpectedly.

High-speed video cameras have been used to film the flying motions of bats, revealing details about the mechanisms of bat flight. The intricate nature of the bats' flight patterns shocked scientists at first because they were so much different than the flight patterns of birds which scientists thought would be similar to bats. Bats never flatten their wings like an airplane when they are flying. Rather the wings of bats curve, curl, and change direction constantly as they fly. Even if airplanes flapped their wings like bats, they still wouldn't be mimicking accurately the flight pattern of bats. <u>That is because the curving and curling of the wing is the key which allows bats to fly the way they do.</u>

Scientists will continue studying the flight pattern of bats in the hope that they can one day be able to design airplanes and other types of flying machines that will fly like bats do. Bat-like flying machines could be a big help fighting in war and in emergency situations like fires, earthquakes, or volcanic eruptions, to rescue people from tight, collapsed spaces or perform other tasks.

| 해석 |

박쥐 세계는 다양함으로 가득하다. 다양한 종류의 박쥐들이 과일에서 곤충에 이르는 다양한 식단을 가지고 있을 뿐만 아니라, 어떤 박쥐들은 돌아다니기 위해 음파를 사용하는 반면, 다른 것들은 눈을 사용한다. 더욱이, 세상의 1200종이 넘는 박쥐들 중, 아주 적은 종들만이 영양 공급을 위해 피를 빤다. 그러나 모든 박쥐들에게 공통적인 것은, 존재하는 포유류 중에서 유일하게 날아다니는 포유류라는 것 말고도, 박쥐들로

하여금 비행 곡예를 하게끔 하는 유연한 날개를 갖고 있다는 점이다. 박쥐는 매우 빠르게 방향을 바꾸거나 회전하면서, 갑작스럽고 예기치 않게 올라갔다 내려갔다 한다.

고속 비디오 카메라를 이용해 박쥐들이 날아다니는 동작을 찍어, 박쥐 비행의 메커니즘에 관한 상세한 사실들을 밝혀냈다. 난해한 박쥐의 비행 패턴은 박쥐들이 새들과 비슷한 비행을 할 것이라고 생각했던 것과 아주 많이 달라서 처음에는 과학자들에게 충격을 주었다. 박쥐들은 날면서 비행기처럼 결코 날개를 평평하게 하지 않는다. 오히려 박쥐의 날개는 날면서 구부리거나 비틀거나 하며 끊임없이 방향을 바꾼다. 비행기가 박쥐처럼 파닥거릴지라도, 여전히 비행기는 박쥐들의 비행 패턴을 정확하게 흉내내지 못할 것이다. 왜냐하면 날개를 구부리고 비트는 것이 박쥐로 하여금 그렇게 날 수 있게 하는 열쇠이기 때문이다.

과학자들은 언젠가는 박쥐가 나는 것처럼 날 수 있을 비행기나 다른 종류의 비행 장치를 설계할 수 있을 것이라는 희망을 가지고 박쥐의 비행 패턴을 계속 연구할 것이다. 박쥐와 같은 비행 장치는 전쟁과 화재나 지진이나 화산 폭발과 같은 위급 상황에서 싸울 때 큰 도움이 될 수 있어서, 좁고 무너진 곳에서 사람들을 구하거나 다른 임무들을 수행할 수 있을 것이다.

| 구문 |

- High-speed video cameras have been used to film the flying motions of bats, revealing details about the mechanisms of bat flight.
  revealing 이하는 결과를 나타내는 분사구문이다.

GRAMMAR Quiz

1. 그는, 내가 믿기로는, 위대한 정치가이다.
   → He is, I believe, a great statesman.

2. 그녀는, 내가 보기에는, 매우 활동적이고 창조적이다.
   → She is, it seems to me, very active and creative.

3. 한번 내뱉은 말은, 일단 발사된 탄환처럼, 회수될 수 없다.
   → Words once spoken, like bullets once fired, can't be recalled.

STRUCTURE

What all bats have in common is, other than being the only flying mammals in existence, flexible wings that allow them to perform flying feats.

◎ 이 문장에서 삽입된 전치사구는?
   → other than being the only flying mammals in existence

◎ 주어 What의 보어가 되는 말은?
   → flexible wings

〈문장의 구조〉

- 주어 → What all bats have in common
- 동사 → is
- (전치사구) → other than being the only flying mammals in existence
- 보어 → flexible wings
- (관계사절) → that allow them to perform flying feats

WRITING

1. Not only do different types of bats have different diets, but also some bats use sound waves to move around.
   (다양한 종류의 박쥐들은 ~을 가지고 있을 뿐만 아니라)

2. What all bats have in common is flexible wings that allow them to perform flying feats.
   (모든 박쥐들이 공통적으로 갖는 것은)

3. They were so much different than the flight patterns of birds which scientists thought would be similar to bats. (박쥐와 비슷할 것이다)

4. Bats never flatten their wings like an airplane when they are flying.
   (날개를 결코 평평하게 하지 않는다)

5. That is because the curving and curling of the wing is the key which allows bats to fly the way they do. (박쥐로 하여금 그들이 하는 그런 방법으로 날 수 있게 하다)

06
Passage

| 정답 |

1. ③
2. ⑤
3. ②
4. 청결과 식사에 대한 엄격한 규율을 통해 자기 수련한다.
   / 5년 동안 침묵 속에서 주요 과목을 공부한다.

| 해설 |

1. It is unknown whether all these rules were imposed by Pythagoras himself or were the products of his followers.라는 문장에서 엄격한 규칙들이 누구에 의해 만들어졌는지 알려져 있지 않다고 했다. 그러므로 ③ Pythagoras made strict rules of self-discipline and study.(피타고라스는 자기훈련과 학업에 엄격한 규칙을 만들었다.)는 내용이 일치하지 않는다.
   다음 중 글의 내용으로 맞지 않은 것은?
   ① 피타고라스는 그 사회에 대단히 큰 정치적 영향력을 행사했다.
   ② 피타고라스와 그의 추종자들은 대단히 존경받았다.
   ④ 피타고라스는 영혼이 다시 태어난다고 믿었다.
   ⑤ 피타고라스는 자신의 학파에 여성을 회원으로 받아들였다.

2. despicable은 「야비한, 비열한」의 의미이다. ⑤의 considerate은 「사려 깊은」이라는 의미로 반대의 뜻이다.
   ① 잔인한   ② 사악한
   ③ 잔인한   ④ 잔혹한

3. 빈칸 앞의 내용은 천체의 움직임이 수학적 규칙에 따라 움직인다는 것이다. 그러므로 빈칸에는 그 규칙에 따라 예측될 수 있다는 ② could be predicted가 가장 적절하다
   ① 벗어나질 수 있다   ③ 다양할 수 있다
   ④ 통제될 수 있다   ⑤ 재배치될 수 있다

4. 피타고라스 학파에 의해 부과된 엄격한 규칙은 '청결과 식사에 대한 엄격한 규율을 통해 자기를 수련하는 것과 5년 동안 침묵 속에서 주요 과목을 공부하는 것' 이었다.
   피타고라스 학파에 의해 부여된 규칙은 무엇인가? (한글로)

| 본문 |

Pythagoras is believed to have journeyed to Egypt, Babylon and then Samos so that he could study advanced mathematics. After a while, he and his devotees left Samos because of political uncertainties and the despicable actions of Samos's tyrant Polikrates. They established a kind of sect in southern Italy. Unlike many other sects of the day, they accepted women as their members who were highly respected in the region.

Since Pythagoras also believed in reincarnation, he was deeply concerned about the preservation of the soul and its purity. The sect wanted to end the process of reincarnation so that the soul could finally be released from the body which was believed to be imprisoning the soul. To achieve release, the sect focused on improving self-discipline by adhering to rigid rules about hygiene and eating. Also, the sect members studied the principal subjects, including mathematics, music, gymnastics and medicine for five years while keeping silent. It is unknown whether all these rules were imposed by Pythagoras himself or were the products of his followers.

In addition, contrary to popular belief, it was not Pythagoras who discovered the famous "sentence of Pythagoras" but the Babylonians. Babylonian astronomers had discovered that the orbits of the bodies in the sky followed mathematical patterns and could be predicted. Pythagoras is also known to have influenced reforms in the political system since the "associations" started by his followers often managed to attain immense political influence in a given territory.

| 해석 |

피타고라스는 진보된 수학을 공부하기 위해 이집트, 바빌론, 그리고 또 사모스를 여행한 것으로 믿어진다. 얼마 후에, 그와 그의 열성당원들은 정치적 불확실성과 사모스의 폭군

Polikrates의 비열한 행동 때문에 사모스를 떠났다. 그들은 남부 이탈리아에 학파 하나를 세웠다. 그 당시의 많은 다른 학파들과는 달리, 그들은 그 지역에서 대단히 존경받는 자기네 회원으로 여성들을 받아들였다.

피타고라스는 또한 환생을 믿었기 때문에, 영혼의 보호와 영혼의 순수에 깊은 관심이 있었다. 그 학파는 영혼을 가두어 두는 것이라 믿어지는 육체에서 영혼이 벗어날 수 있도록 그 환생의 과정을 끝내고 싶어했다. (영혼의) 해방을 이루기 위해서, 그 학파는 청결과 식사에 엄격한 규칙을 고수함으로써 자기훈련을 향상시키는 데 초점을 맞추었다. 또한 그 학파의 회원들은 주요 과목을 공부했는데, 그것은 수학, 음악, 체육, 의학으로, 침묵 가운데서 5년 동안 배웠다. 이 모든 규칙들이 피타고라스 자신에 의해 부과되었는지 아니면 그의 추종자들이 만들어낸 것인지는 알려져 있지 않다.

게다가, 일반적인 믿음과는 달리, 그 유명한 "피타고라스의 정리"를 발견한 것은 피타고라스가 아니라, 바빌론 사람들이었다. 바빌론의 천문학자들은 하늘의 천체 궤도가 수학적 패턴을 따르고 있어서 예측할 수 있다는 것을 발견했었다. 피타고라스는 또한 정치 제도의 개혁에 영향을 미쳤다고 믿어지는데, 그것은 그의 추종자들에 의해 시작된 그 단체들이 종종 주어진 영토 안에서 막대한 정치적 영향을 갖게 되었기 때문이었다.

| 구문 |

- so that he could study advanced mathematics / so that the soul could finally be released from the body

so that은 목적이나 결과의 부사절을 이끌어 '~하기 위해(서), ~하도록' 또는 '그래서, 그 때문에, ~하여(서)'를 표현한다. 구어에서는 that이 종종 생략되기도 한다.

GRAMMAR Quiz

1. 그는 젊었을 때 부유했던 것 같다.
   → He seems to have been rich in his youth.

2. Michael Jordan은 최고의 농구신수였다고 믿어진다.
   → Michael Jordan is believed to have been the best basketball player.

STRUCTURE

The "associations" started by his followers often managed to attain immense political influence in a given territory.

○ associations란 어떤 단체를 말하는가?
   → started by his followers
   → 해석: 그의 추종자들에 의해 시작된 단체들

〈문장의 구조〉
- 주어 → The "associations" started by his followers
- 동사 → often managed
- 목적어 → to attain immense political influence
- (전치사구) → in a given territory

WRITING

1. Unlike many other sects of the day, they accepted women as their members who were highly respected in the region.
   (그 지역에서 대단히 존경받는)

2. Pythagoras also believed in reincarnation.
   (환생을 믿었다)

3. The soul could finally be released from the body. (~에서 벗어나지다)

4. The sect focused on improving self-discipline by adhering to rigid rules about hygiene and eating. (엄격한 규칙을 고수함으로써)

5. It is unknown whether all these rules were imposed by Pythagoras himself or were the products of his followers.
   (~인지 아닌지 알려져 있지 않다)

07
Passage

| 정답 |

1. ③ / ⑤
2. 생활에 필요한 신선한 물을 공급하는 것 / 하수를 흘려버리는 것
3. this sophisticated water distribution system / a (the) system of canals / The engineering marvel of the whole system
4. ④

1. With such a reliable supply of water within the heart of its cities, Romans built fountains, public baths and artificial lakes.에서 ③ Ample water supplies allowed Roman people to build various facilities.(충분한 물의 공급이 로마 사람들로 하여금 다양한 시설을 건설하게 했다.)의 내용을 확인할 수 있다. 또한 the system of canals and pipes had a constant gradient so that clean water flowed in and dirty water flowed out at a steady speed에서 ⑤ The system used a steady slope for the right speed of water flow.(그 시스템은 적절한 속도의 물의 흐름을 위해 완만하게 경사져 있었다.)라는 것을 알 수 있다.

다음 중 이 글의 내용과 일치하는 것은? (2개)
① 로마 수로는 몇몇 전쟁 기간 중 발명되고 개발되었다.
② 물은 도시에 있는 수원에서 각 가정으로 공급되었다.
④ 수로는 흐르는 물의 양의 통제를 조절할 수 있었다.

2. 로마 사람들이 지은 수로의 주요 기능은 receive fresh water and discard dirty water에서 알 수 있듯이, 생활에 필요한 신선한 물의 공급과 하수를 버리는 것이다.

3. 본문에 사용된 로마의 aqueduct를 뜻하는 표현은 this sophisticated water distribution system, a(the) system of canals, The engineering marvel of the whole system이다.

4. sophisticated는 「복잡한, 정교한」의 의미이다. 그러므로 ④ complex와 바꾸어 쓸 수 있다.

| 본문 |

The ancient Romans were excellent civil engineers, constructing colossal buildings which were incredible engineering achievements of their time. While most people are quite familiar with the Colosseum and other Roman architectural achievements, few know about the Roman system of aqueducts.

Aqueducts that carried water into Roman cities allowed Roman citizens living within large cities to enjoy fresh, clear water in a variety of ways. Not only is the supply of fresh water critical to the life of any resident of a large city, but the removal of dirty water is also important. So the Romans built this sophisticated water distribution system to take away dirty, sewage-filled water as well.

The aqueducts the Romans built were really a system of canals. Water originated from a spot from which it flowed naturally, a spring for example. Then they constructed aqueducts to transport the water into the cities. Canals couldn't be built within cities so the Romans used a series of tanks and pipes to ensure that every area within a given city was able to receive fresh water and discard dirty water. The engineering marvel of the whole system was ensuring that the system of canals and pipes had a constant gradient so that clean water flowed in and dirty water flowed out at a steady speed without any assistance.

With such a reliable supply of water within the heart of its cities, the Romans built fountains, public baths and artificial lakes. In Rome alone there were 1,200 fountains, 11 public baths and 2 artificial lakes.

| 해석 |

고대 로마인들은 뛰어난 토목 기술자들이어서, 그 시대에는 엄청난 기술공학의 업적인 거대한 건물들을 세웠다. 대부분의 사람들이 콜로세움과 로마의 다른 건축물들은 상당히 잘 알고 있지만, 로마의 수로(水路)에 대해 알고 있는 사람들은 거의 없다.

로마 도시들로 물을 운반했던 수로는 큰 도시 안에 살고 있는 로마 시민들로 하여금 여러 가지 방법으로 신선하고 깨끗한 물을 사용할 수 있게 했다. 대도시 거주민들이 생활하는 데 있어 신선한 물을 공급하는 것도 꼭 필요하지만, (그에 못지 않게) 오수(오염된 물)를 처리하는 일도 중요하다. 그래서 로마 사람들은 더럽고 오물로 가득한 물을 버리기 위해서도 이 복잡한 수도 보급 시스템을 만들었다.

로마 사람들이 만든 수로는 진정한 운하 시스템이었다. 물은 자연적으로 물이 흐르는 곳, 예를 들면 샘물에서 나왔다. 그래서 그들은 도시에 물을 보내기 위해 수로를 건설했다. 운하는 도시 안에 세워질 수 없어서, 주어진 도시 안의 모든 지역이 깨끗한 물을 받고 더러운 물을 버릴 수 있도록 로마 사람들은 일련의 수조와 파이프를 사용했다. 그 공학적으로 경이로운 전체 시스템은 어떤 도움 없이도 일정한 속도로 깨끗한 물이 들어오고 더러운 물이 빠져나갈 수 있도록 운하와 파이프 시스템이 일정한 기울기를 갖고 있었다.

도시 중심 안으로 물의 이러한 안정적인 공급으로, 로마 사람들은 분수, 공중 목욕탕과 인공 호수를 만들었다. 로마에만 1,200개의 분수, 11개의 공중 목욕탕과 2개의 인공호수가 있었다.

| 구문 |

- Not only is the supply of fresh water critical ~, but the removal of dirty water is also important.
  not only가 문두로 오면서 주어(the supply of fresh water)와 동사(is)가 도치된 문장이다. ⟨not only ~, but (also) ...⟩는 '~뿐만 아니라 … 또한' 이라는 의미이다.

GRAMMAR Quiz

1. 우리는 말하는 것보다 두 배만큼 들을 수 있기 위해서, 두 개의 귀와 하나의 입을 가지고 있다.
   → We have two ears and one mouth so that we can listen twice as much as we speak.

2. We will do our best in order for them to look forward to a bright future.
   → We will do our best so that they can look forward to a bright future.

STRUCTURE

Aqueducts that carried water into Roman cities allowed Roman citizens living within large cities to enjoy fresh, clear water in a variety of ways.

◐ Aqueducts란 어떤 수로를 말하는가?
   → that carried water into Roman cities
   → 해석: 로마 도시들로 물을 운반했던 수로들

◐ Roman citizens이란 어떤 사람들을 말하는가?
   → living within large cities

⟨문장의 구조⟩
- 주어 → Aqueducts that carried water into Roman cities
- 동사 → allowed
- 목적어 → Roman citizens living within large cities
- 목적격보어 → to enjoy fresh, clear water
- (전치사구) → in a variety of ways

WRITING

1. While most people are quite familiar with the Colosseum, few know about the Roman system of aqueducts. (~을 상당히 잘 알고 있다)

2. Not only is the supply of fresh water critical to the life of any resident of a large city, but the removal of dirty water is also important. (~의 공급이 …할 뿐만 아니라)

3. The Romans built this sophisticated water distribution system to take away sewage-filled water as well. (오물로 가득한 물을 버리기 위해서도)

4. Water originated from a spot from which it flowed naturally, a spring for example. (~로부터 자연적으로 물이 흘렀던)

5. The system had a constant gradient so that clean water flowed in and dirty water flowed out at a steady speed without any assistance. (일정한 기울기를 갖고 있었다)

08
Passage

| 정답 |

1. ④
2. 가장 빨리 성장한다. / 먹이의 비용이 저렴하다. / 돌보기 쉽다.
3. 있을지 모르는 유해한 효과들로부터 닭의 몸을 보호하기 위해서 / 약을 수거할 때의 편리성을 위해서
4. ④

| 해설 |

1. 마지막 문장에서 보면, 더 많은 실험이 필요하다고 했으므로 동물로 된 약은 아직 시판되고 있지 않다는 것을 알 수 있다. 그러므로 ④ Harmful side effects have not been found in animal drugs in the market.(시장에 있는 동물 약에서 해로운 효과는 발견되지 않았다.)의 내용은 사실이 아니다.
   이 글에 따르면, 다음 중 사실이 아닌 것은?
   ① 닭을 포함한 몇몇 동물들은 약을 만들어내는 데에 사

용된다.

② 유전학적으로 DNA가 변형된 동물들은 자체적으로 약을 만들어낼 수 있다.

③ 약은 몸체의 많은 부분들의 주요 요소인 단백질로 만들어진다.

⑤ 어떤 동물들은 다양한 약을 만들기 위해 성공적으로 가공되었다.

2. since they grow fastest. Chickens are also cheap to feed and easy to take care of.에서 답을 찾아볼 수 있다. 즉, 가장 빨리 자라고, 먹이의 비용이 저렴하고, 돌보기 쉽기 때문이다.

대량 생산을 위한 동물로 닭이 선호되는 이유를 설명하시오. (우리말로)

3. This protects the chickens' bodies from the drugs' possible harmful effects and makes it easy for scientists to collect the drugs.에 답이 나와 있다. 즉, 있을지 모르는 유해한 효과들로부터 닭의 몸을 보호하고 약을 수거할 때의 편리성을 위해서이다.

4. 약을 만들어 내는 능력(drug creating ability)이 병아리에게 유전된다는 내용을 통해, ④ Changing the DNA of every chicken to make drugs is not necessary.(약을 만들기 위해 모든 닭의 DNA를 바꾸는 것은 필요하지 않다.)라는 것을 추론할 수 있다.

다음 중 이 글에서 추론할 수 있는 것은?

① 약을 만들어내는 능력은 다른 세대로 전해질 수 없다.

② 가까운 장래에 단백질 약으로 대부분의 질병이 치유될 수 있다.

③ 이런 종류의 몇몇 달걀들은 현재 몇몇 동네 시장에서 구할 수 있다.

⑤ 인간의 소비를 위해 충분히 많은 달걀을 만드는 데에는 몇 년이 걸릴 것이다.

| 본문 |

Medicine can come in the form of capsules, tablets or powder which we take with water. It can also come in the form of cream which we apply to our skin. Now scientists are trying to genetically engineer medicines into our food. No longer would you have to take your pills after eating your eggs for breakfast as the eggs would have the medicine already in them.

This is possible because drugs are made of protein molecules. Animals make thousands of proteins, the main ingredient in skin, hair, milk, and meat. If drugs are made from the proteins, then animals can be genetically engineered to produce the drugs themselves.

In fact, sheep, cows and goats have already been genetically engineered by scientists to produce protein drugs which are collected in those animals' milk. Chickens, however, are the best choice to mass produce drugs for human consumption since they grow fastest. Chickens are also cheap to feed and easy to take care of. Since chickens don't produce milk, people would simply eat some eggs to get their needed daily dose of medicine. The scientists altered the chickens' DNA so that the birds make these drugs only in their egg whites. This protects the chickens' bodies from the drugs' possible harmful effects and makes it easy for scientists to collect the drugs.

Researchers in this field have already produced two types of chickens whose eggs contain protein drugs. One produces a drug to treat skin cancer and the other produces a drug to treat multiple sclerosis, a nerve disorder. These researchers have discovered that the chickens pass on to their chicks their drug creating abilities, making the whole project much more economically feasible. Nevertheless, more testing still needs to be done before these 'medicine eggs' reach your local grocery store.

| 해석 |

약은 물과 복용하는 캡슐, 정제 또는 가루약의 형태로 나올 수 있다. 그것은 또한 피부에 바를 수 있는 크림 형태로 나올 수도 있다. 이제 과학자들은 유전학적으로 음식에 약을 넣어 만들려고 노력하고 있다. 이제 더 이상 아침 식사로 달걀을 먹은 후에 약을 복용할 필요가 없을 것인데, 그 달걀에 이미 그 약이 들어 있을 것이기 때문이다.

이것은 약이 단백질 분자로 만들어지기 때문에 가능하다. 동물들은 가죽, 털, 젖, 그리고 고기의 주요 성분인 수천 가지의 단백질을 만든다. 약이 단백질로 만들어진다면, 동물들이 자체로 약을 만들어낼 수 있도록 유전학적으로 가공될 수 있다.

사실, 양, 젖소와 염소는 그 동물들의 젖에서 모아진 단백질 약을 만들어내기 위해서 과학자들에 의해 이미 유전학적으로 가공되어 왔다. 그러나 닭이 가장 빠르게 자라기 때문에 인간의 소비를 위한 약을 대량 생산하기 가장 좋다. 또한 닭은 사료값도 싸고 돌보기도 쉽다. 닭은 우유를 만들어내지 못하기 때문에, 사람들은 약간의 달걀을 먹는 것으로 필요한 매일의 약을 얻을 수 있다. 과학자들은 그 새(즉, 닭)가 이런 약들을 흰자위에만 만들도록 닭의 DNA를 바꾸었다. 이것은 그 약에 잠재되어 있는 유해 효과로부터 닭의 몸을 보호하고 과학자들로 하여금 그 약을 수거하는 것을 쉽게 만든다.

이 분야의 연구원들은 이미 그 달걀에 단백질 약이 포함된 두 가지 종류의 닭을 만들어냈다. 하나는 피부암을 치료하기 위한 약을 만들어내고 다른 것은 신경 장애인 다발성경화증을 치료하는 약을 만들어낸다. 이들 연구원들은 닭이 자신의 새끼들에게 약을 만들어내는 능력을 물려줘서 전체 프로젝트가 훨씬 더 경제적으로 수월하게 한다는 것을 발견했다. 그럼에도 불구하고, '의학용 달걀'이 동네 가게에 공급되기 전에 여전히 더 많은 실험이 행해져야 할 필요가 있다.

| 구문 |

- Medicine can come in the form of capsules, tablets or powder which we take with water. / It can also come in the form of cream which we apply to our skin.
  앞 문장의 which는 take의 목적어로 capsules, tablets or powder를 선행사로 받고 있다. 뒤 문장의 which는 apply의 목적어로 cream이 선행사이다.

- No longer would you have to take your pills
  No longer라는 부정어구가 문두로 나오면서, 주어(you)와 조동사(would)가 도치되었다.

GRAMMAR Quiz

1. 나는 매일 일기를 쓰는 것을 규칙으로 하고 있다.
   → I make it a rule to keep a diary every day.

2. 그녀는 그 문제에 대해서 아무 말도 하지 않는 것이 최선이라고 여겼다.
   → She considered it best to say nothing about the matter.

3. 어떤 톨게이트에서는 컴퓨터가 차량들이 톨게이트를 통과하는 것을 수월하게 해 준다.
   → Computers in some tollgates make it easy

for cars to pass through them.

STRUCTURE

Sheep, cows and goats have already been genetically engineered by scientists to produce protein drugs which are collected in those animals' milk.

◐ to produce는 부정사의 어떤 용법인가?
   → 부사적 용법 (목적)
   → 해석: 생산하기 위하여

◐ protein drugs는 어떤 약을 말하는가?
   → which are collected in those animals' milk
   → 해석: 그 동물들의 젖에서 모아지는 (단백질 약)

〈문장의 구조〉
- 주어 → Sheep, cows and goats
- 동사 → have already been
- 보어 → genetically engineered
- (전치사구) → by scientists
- (부정사구) → to produce protein drugs
- (관계대명사절) → which are collected in those animals' milk

WRITING

1. It can also come in the form of cream which we apply to our skin. (우리가 피부에 바를 수 있는)

2. No longer would you have to take your pills after eating your eggs for breakfast. (더 이상 ~할 필요가 없을 것이다)

3. Chickens are also cheap to feed and easy to take care of. (돌보기 쉬운)

4. The chickens pass on to their chicks their drug creating abilities, making the whole project much more economically feasible.
   (훨씬 더 경제적으로 수월하게)

5. Nevertheless, more testing still needs to be done before these 'medicine eggs' reach your local grocery store.
   (여전히 더 많은 실험이 행해져야 할 필요가 있다)

Review

| A |

01. ~에 집착하다, 고수하다
02. 인공의
03. 야비한, 비열한
04. 열성가
05. 보급, 배분
06. 묘기, 재주, 곡예
07. 경사도, 기울기
08. 위생 상태, 청결함
09. 포유류
10. 흉내내다, 모방하다
11. 환생
12. 확실한, 믿을 수 있는

| B |

01. a reliable friend
02. unbelievable feats
03. artificial flowers
04. the distribution of wealth
05. believe in reincarnation
06. Whales are mammals.

| C |

01. adhere
02. gradient
03. devotee
04. hygiene
05. despicable
06. mimic

| D |

01. ①
02. ②
03. ②
04. ③
05. ③
06. ③
07. ③
08. ①
09. ②
10. ③

Chapter 03

Vocabulary Pre-check

- alertness 각성도
- astronomer 천문학자
- authorial 작가적인, 작가의
- be cloaked in ~으로 덮여 있다
- blistering 굉장한
- cue 단서, 자극
- compelling 강력한, 하지 않을 수 없는
- complication 복잡함
- component 성분, 요소
- composition 구성, 성분
- confusion 혼동, 혼란
- cram 주입시키다, 벼락공부를 하다
- current 현재의
- define 규정짓다, 경계가 뚜렷하다
- deflect 비끼게 하다, 빗나가게 하다
- distinct 별개의, 다른
- dominate 우세하다, 특색지우다
- drift 표류(하다)
- edge 가장자리, 테두리
- emit 방출하다
- extremely 극도로
- flashback 플래시백(과거 회상 장면으로의 전환)
- gadget (간단한) 장치
- giant 거대한
- gravity 중력
- haze 안개, 아지랑이
- imprecise 부정확한
- in response to ~에 반응하여
- infrared 적외선의
- inherit 물려받다
- insights 통찰력
- intermingle 혼합하다, 섞다
- intriguing 호기심을 자아내는
- invisible 보이지 않는
- locale 장소, 현장
- magnet 자석
- maintain 유지시키다
- Mercury 수성

- microscope 현미경
- narrative 이야기(의)
- nod off 꾸벅꾸벅 졸다
- oversized 너무 큰, 특대의
- paradox 역설, 앞뒤가 맞지 않는
- participant 참가자, 참여자
- perplexed 당혹한, 어찌할 바를 모르는
- Pluto 명왕성
- protagonist 주역, 주인공
- radiation 방사성(의)
- reveal 드러내다, 밝혀내다
- seemingly 보기에는
- shepherd 양치기
- subject 피실험자, 실험 대상자
- telescope 망원경
- tension 긴장감
- thematically 주제상으로
- tissue 조직
- unfold 펼치다, 벌리다
- vacuum 진공

WRITE

09
Passage

| 정답 |

1. ⑤
2. • 기존의 X ray: 부정확하여 건강한 조직까지 손상시킬 수 있다.
   • 싱크로트론 X ray: 정확하게 암세포만을 파괴하여 건강한 조직의 손상이 없다.
3. ④
4. ②

| 해설 |

1. 이 글은 싱크로트론(하전 입자 가속 장치)에 관한 내용으로, 자성을 생산하는 것이 아니라, 자성을 이용하여 전자들이 만드는 빛이 빔라인이 되도록 하는 것으로 ⑤ It produces magnetic energy which turns into bright beamlines.(그것은 밝은 빔라인으로 변하는 자성을 띤 에너지를 생산한다.)는 틀린 설명이다.

   이 글에 따르면 싱크로트론에 대해 사실이 아닌 것은?
   ① 그것은 고도로 강력한 광선을 만들어내기 위해 발명되었다.
   ② 그것은 전자가 믿을 수 없을 만큼 빛의 속도에 가깝게 이동하게 한다.
   ③ 그것은 특별한 목적을 위해 특별한 한 종류의 빛을 발산할 수 있다.
   ④ 그것은 목적에 따라 에너지의 양을 조절할 수 있다.

2. 세 번째 단락의 내용으로 보아, 기존의 X ray는 부정확하여 건강한 조직까지 손상시킬 수 있지만, 싱크로트론 X ray는 정확하게 암세포만을 파괴하여 건강한 조직에 손상을 입히지 않고 치료할 수 있다.

3. 필자가 현미경을 언급하는 이유는 싱크로트론이 무엇을 하는 기계인지 쉽게 설명하기 위한 것이다. 그러므로 ④ to help the understanding of the overall purpose of the synchrotron(싱크로트론의 전반적인 용도를 이해하는 데에 도움을 주기 위해)가 정답이다.
   필자가 현미경을 언급하는 이유는 무엇인가?
   ① 싱크로트론의 모양과 그 부품들에 대해 간단한 인상을 주기 위해
   ② 싱크로트론이 현재의 현미경을 대체하게 될 것이라는 점을 암시하기 위해

③ 싱크로트론 기계로 물체들이 어떻게 관찰되는지 보여주기 위해
⑤ 싱크로트론이 지금보다 훨씬 더 작아져야 한다는 점을 설명하기 위해

4. 주어진 문장의 The work는 과학자들이 원자나 세포의 구조를 보다 더 깊이 보기 위해 이 거대한 기계를 사용하고 있는 것이므로 (B)에 위치하는 것이 가장 적절하다.

| 본문 |

A synchrotron is a machine which is as long and wide as a football field. It might be mistaken for an inventor's oversized gadget, but it is not a gadget. It is a powerful machine that uses tubes, magnets, vacuum pumps, and other gadgetry to produce intensely powerful beams of light. Scientists are using this huge machine to look deeper than ever into the structure of atoms and cells. The work is giving them insights into the human body and the world. Everyone knows about microscopes that let you see what the eye can't see, and this is like the next level of microscope.

A synchrotron uses giant magnets, radio waves, and something called an electron gun to push electrons until they move at a blistering 99.9987 percent of the speed of light. Electrons moving that quickly produce extremely bright light. Magnets direct this light into beams, known as beamlines. Each beamline can be designed to emit just one type of light, ranging from infrared to X rays, with a very specific amount of energy.

The synchrotron can be used to treat diseases. For example, doctors often use X rays to kill cancer cells. Radiation treatments are imprecise, however, and many healthy cells die in the process. By using the highly focused synchrotron X-ray beam, scientists hope to destroy individual cancer cells without harming healthy tissue.

Not only can this technology be used by medical companies, but the technology can also be used by food companies for better tasting foods. The synchrotron's X-ray beam was used by a chocolate manufacturer to discover the ideal temperature for processing chocolate.

| 해석 |

싱크로트론은 축구장만큼 길고 넓은 기계이다. 그것은 발명가가 지나치게 크게 만든 간단한 장치라고 오인될지 모르지만, 그것은 간단한 장치가 아니다. 그것은 대단히 강력한 광선을 만들어내기 위해 튜브, 자석, 진공 펌프와 다른 기계 장치들을 사용하는 강력한 기계이다. 과학자들은 원자나 세포의 구조를 그 어느 때보다 더 깊이 보기 위해 이 거대한 기계를 사용하고 있다. 그 일은 그들에게 인간의 몸과 세상에 대한 통찰력(꿰뚫어봄, 이해)을 주고 있다. 모든 사람들은 눈으로 볼 수 없는 것을 보게 하는 현미경에 대해 알고 있고, 이것은 현미경의 그 다음 단계와 같다.

싱크로트론은 빛의 속도의 99.9987퍼센트의 굉장한 속도로 움직일 때까지 전자를 밀어내기 위해 거대한 자석, 전자파, 그리고 전자총이라고 불리는 것들을 사용한다. 그렇게 빠르게 움직이는 전자는 극도로 밝은 빛을 생성한다. 자석은 이 빛을 빔라인이라고 알려진 광선이 되게 한다. 각각의 빔라인은 적외선에서 엑스선에 이르기까지 단 한 종류의 빛만을 아주 일정한 에너지 양만큼 발사하도록 설계될 수 있다.

싱크로트론은 질병을 치료하기 위해 사용될 수 있다. 예를 들면, 의사들은 암 세포를 죽이기 위해 자주 엑스선을 사용한다. 하지만 방사선 치료는 부정확해서 그 과정에서 많은 건강한 세포들이 죽는다. 고도로 정확한 싱크로트론 엑스선 광선을 사용함으로써, 과학자들은 건강한 조직에 해를 입히지 않고 암세포들을 하나하나 파괴하게 되기를 희망한다.

이 기술은 의학계에 의해 사용될 뿐만 아니라 더 맛있는 식품을 위해 식품회사에 의해 사용될 수도 있다. 싱크로트론의 엑스선 광선은 초콜릿 가공을 위한 이상적인 온도를 알아내기 위해 초콜릿 제조업자에 의해 사용되었다.

| 구문 |

• A synchrotron is a machine which is as long and wide as a football field. / It is a powerful machine that uses tubes, magnets, vacuum pumps, and other gadgetry

앞 문장의 which와 뒤 문장의 that은 둘 다 주격 관계대명사이다. which는 a machine을, that은 a powerful machine을 받는다. 한편 앞 문장의 as long and wide as a football field은 원급을 이용한 비교문장이다.

• Everyone knows about microscopes that let you see what the eye can't see

that은 주격 관계대명사로 microscopes를 받으며, 사역동사 let이 목적어 you와 목적격보어로 원형부정사 see를 취하고 있다. what the eye can't see는 see의 목적어이다.

GRAMMAR Quiz

1. 우리는 먹기 위해 사는 것이 아니라 살기 위해서 먹는다.
   → We do not live to eat, but eat to live.

2. 어느 날 아침, 잠에서 깨어 유명해져 있는 나 자신을 발견했다.
   → One morning I awoke to find myself famous.

STRUCTURE

A synchrotron uses giant magnets, radio waves, and something called an electron gun to push electrons until they move at a blistering 99.9987 percent of the speed of light.

❍ A synchrotron이 사용하는 것을 모두 쓰시오.
   → giant magnets
   → radio waves
   → something called an electron gun

〈문장의 구조〉
• 주어   → A synchrotron
• 동사   → uses
• 목적어   → giant magnets, radio waves, and something called an electron gun
• (부정사구) → to push electrons until they move ~ the speed of light

WRITING

1. A synchrotron is a machine which is as long and wide as a football field. (~만큼 길고 넓은)

2. Scientists are using this huge machine to look deeper than ever into the structure of atoms and cells. (그 어느 때보다 더 깊이 보기 위해)

3. Everyone knows about microscopes that let you see what the eye can't see. (눈으로 볼 수 없는 것을 당신이 보게 하다)

4. Each beamline can be designed to emit just one type of light, ranging from infrared to X rays, with a very specific amount of energy. (적외선에서 엑스선에 이르기까지)

5. Not only can this technology be used by medical companies, but the technology can also be used by food companies for better tasting foods. (이 기술은 사용될 수 있을 뿐만 아니라)

Passage 10

| 정답 |

1. ③
2. less sleep / long forms / more sleep
3. ④
4. ②

| 해설 |

1. So, you may have two longs, two shorts, or one of each.에서 보면, 수면 유전자는 두 개인데, 두 개 다 길거나 두 개 다 짧거나 각각 하나씩일 것이다. 그러므로 ③ A person might have one long and one short Period 3 gene.(어떤 사람은 Period 3 유전자가 하나는 길고 하나는 짧을 수 있다.)이 옳다.
이 글에 따르면, 다음 중 옳은 것은?
① 모든 사람은 긴 Period 3 유전자를 적어도 하나 가지고 있다.
② Period 3 유전자의 결합은 성장하면서 변할 수 있다.
④ Period 3 유전자를 포함하는 시계 유전자에는 많은 종류가 있다.
⑤ Period 3 유전자는 기본적으로 나이가 들면서 더 길어진다.

2. period 3 유전자가 짧은 사람들이 긴 사람들보다 더 적은 수면을 필요로 한다는 내용이므로, 다음과 같이 정리할 수 있다.
→ A person with short forms of the Period 3 gene needs less sleep, while a person with long forms requires more sleep to have their brains work at top form. (Period 3 유전자가 짧은 형태의 사람은 더

적은 수면을 필요로 한다, 반면에 긴 형태의 사람은 자기 뇌를 최상의 상태에서 작동시키려면 더 많은 잠을 필요로 한다.)

3. 주어진 문장의 For example로 보아 실험의 한 예라는 것을 알 수 있다. 그러므로 실험을 했다는 문장 뒤인 (D)의 위치가 가장 적절하다.

4. perplexed는 「당혹한, 어찌할 바를 모르는」이라는 의미이므로, 이 뜻과 가장 가까운 단어는 ② puzzled이다.

| 본문 |

Bill was up all night cramming for a biology test at school. Sue was too. Sue, however, didn't nod off during the test while Bill did. While this might seem like a paradox, researchers have known for a long time that different people have different sleep requirements. What has always perplexed researchers is why people have these different requirements. What they are now discovering is that our need for sleep has a genetic component. So Bill who received the F can only blame his parents for falling asleep during a test, while Sue has to go home and thank hers.

Researchers have recently discovered that one gene, the "clock gene," affects how well a person functions without sleep. It is a type of gene called a Period 3 gene. The Period 3 gene comes in two forms: short and long. Everyone has two copies of the gene. So you may have two longs, two shorts, or one of each. The forms a person has depend on what he or she inherited from his or her parents.

In a recent study, scientists studied test subjects who had stayed awake for 40 hours straight. Then, these participants did a variety of tests to measure their mental alertness. For example, researchers tested how quickly they pushed a button in response to a visual cue. The results revealed that people who have short forms of this gene do much better with less or no sleep than people who have the long forms of the gene. The researchers concluded that people with the long form of the Period 3 gene dealing with sleep simply needed more sleep to keep their brains working well.

| 해설 |

Bill은 학교 생물학 시험을 위해서 밤새 벼락치기로 공부했다. Sue도 마찬가지였다. Bill은 시험 시간 동안 졸았지만, Sue는 졸지 않았다. 이것은 앞뒤가 맞지 않은 것처럼 보일지도 모르지만, 연구진은 서로 다른 사람들이 서로 다른 수면을 필요로 한다는 것을 오랫동안 알고 있었다. 연구진을 언제나 당혹스럽게 했던 것은 왜 사람들이 서로 다른 수면을 필요로 하느냐는 것이다. 이제 그들이 알아내고 있는 것은 수면에 대한 우리의 요구가 유전자적 요소라는 것이다. 그래서 F를 받은 Bill은 시험 시간 동안 잠들어버린 것에 대해 부모님을 탓할 수 있고, 반면에 Sue는 집으로 가서 부모님께 감사해야 한다.

최근 연구진은 "시계 유전자"라는 한 유전자가 잠을 자지 않고도 사람이 얼마나 잘 움직일 수 있는지에 영향을 미친다는 것을 발견해냈다. 그것은 Period 3 유전자라 불리는 일종의 유전자이다. Period 3 유전자는 짧은 것과 긴 것, 두 가지 형태가 있다. 모든 사람은 이 유전자를 두 개 가지고 있다. 그러니까 두 개 다 길거나 두 개 다 짧거나 각각 하나씩일 것이다. 개인이 가지는 유전자 형태는 부모에게서 물려받기 나름이다.

최근 연구에서, 과학자들은 40시간 동안 줄곧 깨어 있었던 실험 대상자들을 연구했다. 그때 이 참여자들은 정신적인 각성도를 측정하기 위해 다양한 테스트를 받았다. 예를 들면, 연구진은 그들이 시각적인 자극에 반응하여 얼마나 빠르게 버튼을 누르는지 실험했다. 결과는 이 유전자가 짧은 사람들이 그 유전자가 긴 사람들보다 잠이 모자라거나 자지 않아도 훨씬 더 잘한다는 것을 밝혀냈다. 연구진은 수면을 조절하는 Period 3 유전자의 길이가 긴 사람들이 두뇌가 잘 돌아가기 위해 더 많은 잠을 필요로 한다고 결론 내렸다.

| 구문 |

- What has always perplexed researchers is why people have these different requirements. / What they are now discovering is that our need for sleep has a genetic component.
  두 문장은 주어 what절, 동사 is, 보어로 각각 why절과 that절을 취하고 있다.
- one gene, the "clock gene," affects how well a person functions without sleep

one gene과 the "clock gene"은 동격이며 동사 affects의 목적어로 간접의문문이 온 형태이다.

- The forms (that) a person has / depend on / what he or she inherited from his or her parents.
  (that) a person has는 주어 The forms를 수식하며, 동사는 depend on, 목적어로 what절이 온 문장이다.

GRAMMAR Quiz

1. 이 꽃들은 저 꽃들보다 덜 예쁘지는 않다.
   → These flowers are not less beautiful than those flowers.
2. 말의 타격은 칼의 타격보다 훨씬 더 심한 충격을 준다.
   → A blow with a word strikes even deeper than a blow with a sword.

STRUCTURE

What has always perplexed researchers is why people have these different requirements.

❍ What과 동격인 것을 쓰시오.
   → 동격: why people have these different requirements

- 동격을 주어에 대입하여 문장을 다시 쓰시오.
   → Why people have these different requirements has always perplexed researchers.

〈문장의 구조〉

- 주어 → What has always perplexed researchers
- 동사 → is
- 보어 → why people have these different requirements

WRITING

1. Bill was up all night cramming for a biology test at school. (밤새 벼락치기 공부를 하느라 깨어 있었다)
2. What they are now discovering is that our need for sleep has a genetic component. (이제 그들이 발견하고 있는 것은)
3. Researchers have recently discovered that one gene, the "clock gene," affects how well a person functions without sleep. (사람이 얼마나 잘 움직이는지[작동하는지])

4. The forms a person has depend on what he or she inherited from his or her parents.
(사람이 가지는 형태들은)

5. In a recent study, scientists studied test subjects who had stayed awake for 40 hours straight. (40시간 동안 줄곧 깨어 있었던)

Passage 11

| 정답 |

1. ②
2. 연관 없어 보이는 두세 가지 이야기를 동시에 이야기한다. / 이야기 속에 또 다른 이야기를 전개해 나간다. / 과거 또는 과거의 회상과 현재를 오가며 이야기를 전개한다.
3. 일관된 주제를 유지한다.
4. ④

| 해설 |

1. 사건들이 독자가 초점을 맞출 수 있도록 특별한 장소에서 정말 특별한 시간의 틀 안에서 일어난다고 되어 있으므로 ② Each story should not have many different settings.(각각의 이야기에는 많은 다른 배경을 가지고 있지 말아야 한다.)가 정답이다.
   두 번째 단락에 따르면, 다음 중 사실인 것은?
   ① 각각의 이야기는 하나씩 전개되어야 한다.
   ③ 등장인물들은 서로 다른 이야기들 속에서 종종 뒤섞여 있다.
   ④ 다른 이야기들의 배경은 동일하다.
   ⑤ 다른 이야기들이 매우 비슷한 사건을 포함할 것이다.

2. 이 글은 One, Another, Novelists also alter ~의 순서로 complex narrative를 만드는 방법을 설명하는 글이다. 첫 번째 단락에서는 연관 없어 보이는 두세 가지 이야기를 동시에 이야기하는 방법, 두 번째 단락에서는 이야기 속에 또 다른 이야기를 전개해 나가는 방법, 세 번째 단락에서는 과거 또는 과거의 회상과 현재를 오가며 이야기를 전개하는 방법이 소개되어 있다.

3. 첫 번째 방법의 the stories must be connected thematically, 두 번째 방법의 The stories are tied together not only by a protagonist but by thematic unity, 세 번째 방법의 was able to maintain the theme of the story로 보아 이 글에 소개된 3가지 방법의 공통점은 일관된 주제를 유지하는 것임을 알 수 있다.

4. protagonist는 「주역, 주인공」이라는 뜻이다. 그러므로 ④ leading character와 바꾸어 쓸 수 있다. 앞부분에 the central characters ~ are the same에서 그 뜻을 유추할 수 있다.
   ① 이야기의 독자   ② 이야기 자체
   ③ 이야기 작가   ⑤ 이야기의 배역

| 본문 |

Novelists use many complex narrative structures to build tension and make stories more interesting for readers. And there are several authorial methods of achieving this.

One narrative structure or writing technique involves telling two or three different, seemingly unrelated stories, at the same time. Each story has different characters and is set in a different location. As a result, the jumping back and forth amongst the settings and characters can cause confusion for readers. Therefore time and place are usually clearly defined: events often occur within a very specific time frame in a specific locale to keep the reader focused. While the characters and locales in each story are not intermingled, the stories must be connected thematically.

Another complex narrative structure is the story within a story in which one central character is involved in several stories at the same time. While the central characters and the setting are the same in each story, different events are unfolding in each story. The stories are tied together not only by a protagonist but by thematic unity. Don Quixote is thought to be the first novel which employed this technique.

Novelists also alter the traditional time frame in order to make stories more interesting. The time frame can be altered by adding flashbacks. Or, as it was done by Emily Bronte in *Wuthering Heights*, the whole story can move backward and then forward, again and again, unfolding a compelling and intriguing drama. By using the complex narrative structure, Bronte was able to show how the past and the present are intermingled, and was able to maintain the theme of the story while adding interest by adding complication.

| 해석 |

소설가들은 독자들을 위해 긴장감을 만들어내고 이야기를 더욱 흥미롭게 만들기 위해 여러 복잡한 이야기 구조를 이용한다. 그리고 이것을 이루어내는 작가적 기법들이 몇 가지 있다.

(그 중) 한 가지 이야기 구조 또는 집필 기술은 겉보기에는 연관이 없는 두세 가지 다른 이야기들을 동시에 다루는 것이다. 각각의 이야기는 다른 등장인물들이 있고 다른 배경이 설정된다. 그 결과, 배경과 등장인물들 사이를 넘나드는 것은 독자에게 혼란을 가져다줄 수 있다. 그래서 일반적으로 시간과 공간이 명확하게 한정된다. 즉 종종 사건은 독자가 초점을 맞출 수 있도록 특별한 장소에서 정말 특별한 시간의 틀 안에서 일어난다. 각각의 등장인물들과 장소들은 섞이지 않지만, 이야기는 주제상으로는 연결되어 있어야 한다.

또 다른 복잡한 이야기 구조는 한 중심 등장인물이 동시에 여러 이야기에 관련되어 있는 이야기 안의 이야기이다. 각이야기 안에서 중심 등장인물들과 배경은 동일한 반면, 각이야기 안에서 다른 사건들이 펼쳐지고 있다. 그 이야기들은 주인공에 의해서뿐만 아니라 주제적인 통일에 의해서도 서로 묶여 있다. 돈키호테가 이 기법이 사용된 첫 번째 소설이라고 생각된다.

소설가들은 또한 이야기를 더 재미있게 하기 위해서 전통적인 시간의 구조를 바꾸기도 한다. 시간의 구조는 플래시백(과거 회상 장면으로의 전환)을 더함으로써 바뀔 수 있다. 즉, 에밀리 브론테가 쓴 『폭풍의 언덕』에서 그랬던 것처럼, 이야기 전체가 앞뒤로 반복하여 왔다갔다 하면서, 강력하게 흥미를 돋우는 드라마로 펼쳐질 수 있다. 그 복잡한 이야기 구조를 사용함으로써, 브론테는 과거와 현재가 어떻게 서로 연결되어 있는지를 보여 줄 수 있었고, 복잡함을 더함으로써 흥미를 더하면서 이야기의 주제를 유지시켜 나갈 수 있었다.

| 구문 |

- While the characters and locales in each story are not intermingled / the stories must be connected thematically / The time frame can be

altered by adding flashbacks. / as it was done by Emily Bronte in *Wuthering Heights*
모두 행위를 당하는 수동태 문장이다.

- the whole story can move backward and then forward, again and again, unfolding a compelling and intriguing drama
unfolding 이하는 분사구문이다.

GRAMMAR Quiz

1. 인터넷은 세계를 하나의 세계적 사회로 만들고 있다.
   → The Internet is making the world a global society.

2. 나는 나의 소망이 여러분들 안에서 자라나기를 바란다.
   → I want my hope to grow in you.

STRUCTURE

One narrative structure or writing technique involves telling two or three different, seemingly unrelated stories, at the same time.

○ stories를 수식하는 말들을 모두 쓰시오.
   → two or three different
   → seemingly unrelated
   → 해석: 두세 가지 다른, 겉보기에는 연관이 없는 이야기들

〈문장의 구조〉

- 주어   → One narrative structure or writing technique
- 동사   → involves
- 목적어   → telling two or three different, seemingly unrelated stories
- (전치사구) → at the same time

WRITING

1. Each story <u>has different characters</u> and is set in a different location. (다른 등장인물들을 가지고 있다)

2. While the characters and locales in each story are not intermingled, the stories <u>must be connected thematically</u>.
(주제상으로는 연결되어 있어야 한다)

3. The stories are tied together <u>not only by a protagonist</u> but by thematic unity.
(주인공에 의해서뿐만 아니라)

4. The time frame can be altered by adding flashbacks. (~함으로써 바뀔 수 있다)

5. Bronte was able to show how the past and the present are intermingled.
(과거와 현재가 어떻게 섞여 있는지)

Passage 12

| 정답 |

1. ① / ④
2. 평면인 토성의 고리가 각도에 따라 보였다 안보였다 하기 때문에
3. 양치기 위성의 궤도 가까이 떠돌아다니는 물질이 고리로 다시 돌려보내지거나 위성 그 자체로 끌려들어가기 때문에
4. ④

| 해설 |

1. ① Titan is the only moon in the solar system that is bigger than Mercury.(타이탄은 수성보다 큰 태양계에서 유일한 위성이다.)의 언급은 없다. ④ There are many small shepherd moons that are orbiting the moon Titan.(위성 타이탄의 주위를 돌고 있는 많은 작은 양치기 위성들이 있다.)은 양치기 위성들은 타이탄이 아니라 토성의 위성이다.
다음 중 옳지 않은 것은? (2개)
② 타이탄은 짙은 대기를 가지고 있고 짙은 안개로 싸여 있다.
③ 타이탄의 대기는 생명이 시작되기 전의 지구의 대기와 매우 비슷하다.
⑤ 타이탄의 기후는 지구의 기후와 비슷하다는 것이 밝혀졌다.

2. 첫 번째 단락 마지막 문장 At certain angles the rings are invisible, while at other angles they are clearly visible.에 토성이 때때로 다르게 보이는 이유가 나타나 있다. 즉, 평면인 토성의 고리가 각도에 따라 보였다 안보였다 하기 때문이다.

3. 양치기 위성들이 고리의 가장자리 윤곽을 뚜렷하게 하는데, 그 이유는 material that drifts closer to the

shepherd moons' orbits is either deflected back into the body of the rings or pulled into the moons themselves에 나타나 있다. 즉, 양치기 위성 궤도 가까이 떠돌아다니는 물질이 고리로 다시 돌려보내지거나 위성 그 자체로 끌려들어가기 때문에 고리가 더 좁아지거나 넓혀지지 않고 균형을 이루며 선명한 외곽선을 지니고 있는 것이다.
양치기 위성들이 고리의 가장자리 윤곽을 어떻게 뚜렷하게 하는가? (우리말로)

4. It's covered with white ice that reflects sunlight like freshly fallen snow.에서 답을 찾을 수 있다. 엔켈라두스가 빛나는 이유는 ④ the surface with white ice that reflects sunlight(태양빛을 반사하는 하얀 얼음으로 덮여 있는 표면)이다.
다음 중 엔켈라두스가 빛나는 이유로 언급된 것은?
① 태양처럼 밝은 표면의 절반
② 대부분의 태양빛을 반사하는 깨끗하게 떨어지는 눈
③ 미국의 주(州) 하나만큼 넓은 표면
⑤ 깨끗한 눈으로 덮여 있는 표면

| 본문 |

Galileo Galilei, who was the first to use a telescope, wondered why Saturn sometimes looked different. Astronomers have now proven that the answer lies in the angle at which we view the plane of rings. At certain angles the rings are invisible, while at other angles they are clearly visible.

Astronomers are fascinated not only by Saturn's rings, but also by the 34 known moons, especially Titan, the largest moon orbiting Saturn. Bigger than Mercury and Pluto, Titan is intriguing because it is cloaked in a thick, smog-like haze and has its own atmosphere. Scientists believe that the atmosphere of early Earth was similar in composition to the current atmosphere on Titan. The climate, including wind and rain, creates surface features that are similar to those on Earth and like Earth, is dominated by seasonal weather patterns.

There are several small moons orbiting Saturn as well. A few, such as Pan, Atlas, Prometheus, and Pandora, which orbit near the outer edges of the rings or within gaps in the rings are known as "shepherd moons." The gravity of shepherd moons serves to maintain a sharply defined edge to the rings; material that drifts closer to the shepherd moons' orbits is either deflected back into the body of the rings or pulled into the moons themselves.

One moon, Enceladus, is one of the shiniest objects in the solar system. It's covered with white ice that reflects sunlight like freshly fallen snow. It's about as wide as Arizona. Another interesting moon orbiting Saturn is called Iapetus which has two distinct halves. One is as black as asphalt and the other is as bright as snow. All of Saturn's moons are unique and intriguing science targets.

| 해석 |

갈릴레오 갈릴레이는 망원경을 사용한 첫 번째 사람이었는데, 토성은 왜 가끔 다르게 보이는지 궁금해했다. 천문학자들은 이제 그 해답이 우리가 고리의 평면을 볼 때의 각도에 달려 있다는 것을 알게 되었다. 어떤 각도에서는 고리가 보여지지 않는 반면, 다른 각도에서는 분명하게 보이는 것이다.

천문학자들은 토성의 고리뿐 아니라, 또한 34개의 알려진 위성, 특히 토성의 궤도를 도는 가장 큰 위성인 타이탄에 매료되어 있다. 수성과 명왕성보다 더 큰, 타이탄은 두꺼운 스모그 같은 안개로 덮여 있고 자체 대기를 가지고 있기 때문에 흥미롭다. 과학자들은 초기 지구의 대기가 타이탄의 현재 대기의 구성과 비슷했다고 믿는다. 바람과 비를 포함하는 기후는 지구의 표면 특징들과 비슷한 표면 특징들을 만들어내고, 지구처럼 계절적 기후 패턴의 특색을 지니고 있다.

토성 궤도를 도는 몇몇 작은 위성들도 있다. 고리의 외곽 끝 근처나 고리 사이의 틈새 안에서 궤도를 도는 판, 아틀라스, 프로메테우스, 그리고 판도라처럼 작은 몇몇은 "양치기 위성"이라고 알려져 있다. 양치기 위성들의 중력은 고리의 가장자리가 윤곽이 뚜렷하게 유지되도록 하는데, 양치기 위성의 궤도 가까이를 떠도는 물질이 고리로 다시 돌려보내지거나 위성 그 자체로 끌려들어가기 때문이다.

엔켈라두스라는 위성은 태양계에서 가장 밝은 물질들 중의 하나이다. 그것은 깨끗하게 떨어지는 눈처럼 태양빛을 반사하는 하얀 얼음으로 덮여 있다. 그것은 애리조나 크기만하다. 토성을 도는 또 다른 흥미로운 위성은 뚜렷하게 구분되는 두

개의 절반으로 나누어진 이아페투스라고 불리는 것이다. 한 쪽은 아스팔트처럼 어둡고 다른 반 쪽은 눈처럼 환하다. 토성의 위성 모두는 특별하고 호기심을 자아내는 과학 대상이다.

| 구문 |

• Galileo Galilei wondered why Saturn sometimes looked different.

wonder의 목적어로 간접의문문 why절이 왔다. 간접의문문의 어순은 〈의문사＋주어＋동사〉임에 유의한다.

• At certain angles the rings are invisible, while at other angles they are clearly visible.

부사구 도치 구문이다. 원래 The rings are invisible at certain angles, while they are clearly visible at other angles.에서 부사구가 앞으로 나간 것이다. 주어와 동사의 어순은 바뀌지 않았다.

GRAMMAR Quiz

1. 공기는 수질만큼 심하게 오염되었다.
   → The air is as badly polluted as the water.

2. 어떤 문제에 대한 답을 아는 것은 그 문제를 이해하는 것만큼 중요하지 않다.
   → Knowing the answer to a question is not as (so) important as understanding the question.

STRUCTURE

A few, such as Pan, Atlas, Prometheus, and Pandora, which orbit near the outer edges of the rings or within gaps in the rings are known as "shepherd moons."

🔾 a few의 예로 언급된 것은?
   → Pan, Atlas, Prometheus, and Pandora

🔾 a few란 어떤 위성들을 말하는가?
   → which orbit near the outer edges of the rings or within gaps in the rings
   → 해석: 고리의 외각 끝 근처나 고리들 사이에서 공전하는 몇몇 위성들

〈문장의 구조〉
• 주어 → A few, such as Pan, Atlas, Prometheus, and Pandora, which orbit ~ in the rings
• 동사 → are

- 보어 → known
- (전치사구) → as "shepherd moons"

WRITING

1. Galileo Galilei, who was the first to use a telescope, wondered <u>why Saturn sometimes looked different.</u> (토성이 왜 가끔 다르게 보였는지)

2. <u>At certain angles the rings are invisible,</u> while at other angles they are clearly visible.
(어떤 각도에서는 고리가 보이지 않는다)

3. Scientists believe that the atmosphere of early Earth was <u>similar in composition</u> to the current atmosphere on Titan. (구성에 있어서 비슷했다)

4. The climate creates surface features that are <u>similar to those on Earth.</u>
(지구의 그것들(특징들)과 비슷한)

5. One is as black as asphalt and <u>the other is as bright as snow.</u> (다른 한 쪽은 눈처럼 환하다)

Review

| A |

01. 각도
02. 벼락 치기로 공부하다
03. 별개의, 다른
04. 우세하다, 특색지우다
05. 부정확한
06. 물려받다
07. 호기심을 자아내는
08. 현미경
09. 명왕성
10. 주역, 주인공
11. 망원경
12. 펼치다, 벌리다

| B |

01. at some angles
02. unfold the newspaper
03. imprecise information
04. a protagonist of a modern play
05. Habits are inherited.
06. We are distinct from animals.

| C |

01. intriguing
02. telescope
03. microscope
04. cramming
05. dominate
06. Pluto

| D |

01. ①
02. ①
03. ③
04. ②
05. ③
06. ②
07. ①
08. ②
09. ②
10. ②

Chapter 04

Vocabulary Pre-check

- active 특효 있는
- acute 급성의, 날카로운
- astronomer 천문학자
- bark 껍질
- compound 합성물, 혼합물
- conscious 의식의, 의식있는
- contract 수축하다
- craft 기술
- demonstrate 증명하다
- disorder 장애, 이상
- diverse 다양한
- drastic 격렬한, 강렬한
- dyeing 염색
- effect 초래하다, 가져오다
- emission 발산
- emit 발산하다
- endeavor 노력, 시도
- eventually 결국은
- expand 팽창하다
- expertise 전문 기술
- fabric 직물
- fungus 버섯, 균류
- hydrogen 수소
- hypnosis 최면(술)
- hypnotherapy 최면요법
- illuminate 비추다, 광채를 더하다
- inevitably 불가피하게, 확실히
- ingredient 성분
- irritate 자극하다, 염증을 일으키다
- lighthearted 쾌활한, 마음 편한
- liken 비유하다, 견주다
- manufacture 제조(하다)
- microbe 미생물, 세균
- nebula 성운
- nitrogen 질소
- oxygen 산소
- paralysis 마비
- pay attention to ~에 주의를 기울이다

- penetrate 침투하다, 관통하다
- pharmaceutical 제약의
- planetary 행성의
- potential 잠재적인, 가능성이 있는
- prevail 우세하다, 이기다
- prevalent 널리 보급된
- psychologically 심리학적으로
- relieve 덜다, 가라앉히다
- remnant 잔존물, 나머지
- represent 나타내다, 표시하다
- rheumatism 류머티즘
- snowflake 눈송이
- subconscious 잠재의식(의)
- suspect 의심(하다)
- synonymous 동의어의, 같은 뜻의
- synthesize 합성하다
- take up ~에 착수하다
- trance 혼수상태
- trick 마술, 장난, 속임수
- ultraviolet 자외선
- weaving 직조
- willow 버드나무

13
Passage

| 정답 |

1. ② / ⑤
2. craft / expertise
3. 연습을 통해 배울 수 있다. / 즐거운 오락으로 사용될 수 있다.
4. ②

| 해설 |

1. 최면은 과학이고 기술일 수 있다는 것이 이 글의 주된 내용이므로, ② Hypnosis is merely a trick which some

skilled people can play.(최면은 숙련된 사람들이 행할 수 있는 단순한 마술이다.)은 옳지 않다. 또한 ⑤ Many scientists hesitate to accept hypnosis as part of any scientific field.(많은 과학자들이 최면을 과학 분야의 일종으로 받아들이기를 주저한다.)는 언급되지 않았다.

다음 중 옳지 않은 것은? (2개)

① 최면은 다양한 정신적 문제를 가진 사람들을 치료하기 위해 사용될 수 있다.

③ 어떤 사람이라도 연습을 통해 최면을 걸 수 있는 능력을 익힐 수 있다.

④ 최면은 행동에 영향을 미치는 잠재의식을 다룬다.

2. 여기서 art는 「기술」의 의미이고, 본문에 사용된 같은 의미의 단어로는 craft, expertise가 있다.

3. 세 번째 문단의 because it can be learned through practice as magic can과 because individuals with the expertise can use it for lighthearted entertainment에서 답을 알 수 있다. 즉, Hypnosis가 art인 이유는 연습을 통해 배울 수 있고 즐거운 오락으로 사용될 수도 있기 때문이다.

4. 최면은 정신 치료를 위해 사용되면 과학이고, 즐거움을 위해 사용되면 기술일 수 있다는 것이 이 글의 내용이므로 ② Hypnosis can be either a science or a craft depending on how it is used.(최면은 어떻게 이용되느냐에 따라 과학이나 기술이 될 수 있다.)가 정답이다.

다음 중 이 글에서 추론할 수 있는 것은?

① 평범한 사람이 최면술을 마스터하는 것은 거의 불가능하다.

③ 초보자조차도 몇 번의 시도 후에 사람들을 최면에 거는 데 성공할 수 있다.

④ 최면은 많은 국가에서 다양한 분야의 의학으로 행해지고 있다.

⑤ 최면은 잠재의식을 범죄 수사에 도입하기 위해 주로 사용된다.

| 본문 |

The magician asks a member of the audience to join him on stage for his next trick, hypnotizing someone so that he or she will do something funny. The audience member feeling he or she cannot be hypnotized jumps on the stage. Inevitably the magician prevails. The person falling into a hypnotic trance speaks and possibly reveals something best left unrevealed. Since he is a magician, are we to think that hypnosis is a form of magic? Or is hypnosis a scientific endeavor? Perhaps it is a combination of both these things.

Psychologically speaking, hypnotherapy is a proven method of treating various psychological disorders. It can be used to control our brains so that we alter our behavior. Research has shown that the conscious mind is controlled by our unconscious mind, which is really the driving force behind all our thoughts and behaviors. Hypnosis is a scientific method which allows us to enter the subconscious in order to reprogram desires and effect behavior changes.

Hypnosis is also part art because it can be learned through practice as magic can. Hypnosis has been likened to playing a musical instrument. While we may have a talent to hypnotize, we will never be able to actually do it unless we practice it. Hypnotherapy is also a craft because individuals with the expertise can use it for lighthearted entertainment. Stage hypnosis is practiced successfully by many professionals, who manage to make people laugh even while demonstrating how powerful our subconscious really is.

| 해석 |

마술사가 그의 다음 마술을 위해 재미있는 무언가를 할 수 있도록 누군가에게 최면을 걸테니 무대에 함께 해달라고 관중에게 요청한다. 최면에 걸리지 않을 거라고 느끼는 한 관중이 무대로 뛰어올라간다. (그러나) 마술사는 (관중을 압도해) 최면에 빠뜨린다. 최면상태에 빠진 그 사람은 말을 해서 감춰두는 게 최선인 무언가를 말하게 될 수도 있다. 그가 마술사이기 때문에, 우리는 최면이 마술의 종류라고 생각해야 하는가? 아니면 최면은 과학적 시도인가? 아마도 그것은 이 두 가지가 합쳐진 것일 것이다.

심리학적으로 말하면, 최면요법은 다양한 심리적인 장애를 치료하는 수단이라고 증명되었다. 그것은 우리의 뇌를 통제해서 우리가 행동을 바꾸는 데에 사용될 수 있다. 연구가 보여 주는 것은, 의식은 무의식에 의해 통제되는데, 무의식은 우리의 모든 생각과 행동 너머에서 (의식에 대한) 견인차 역할을 한다. 최면은 욕망을 다시 프로그램하고 행동 변화를 유발하기 위해 우리를 잠재의식 속으로 들어가게 해 주는 과학적 방법이다.

최면은 또한 마술처럼 연습을 통해 학습할 수 있는 것이기 때문에 부분적으로 기술이다. 최면은 악기를 연주하는 것에 비유되어 왔다. 우리가 최면을 거는 능력을 가지고 있더라도, 연습하지 않으면 실제로 결코 할 수 없을 것이다. 최면요법은 그 전문 기술을 지닌 개인이 즐거운 오락으로 사용할 수 있기 때문에 또한 기술이다. 무대 위에서의 최면은 많은 전문가들에 의해 성공적으로 행해지고 있는데, 그 전문가들은 우리의 잠재의식이 정말 얼마나 강력한지 증명하면서도 사람들을 웃게 만든다.

| 구문 |

- it can be learned through practice as magic can (be learned)

as magic can 뒤에는 앞에 나온 be learned가 생략되었다. 반복되는 어구는 생략되는 경향이 있다.

- we will never be able to actually do it unless we practice it

조건이나 시간을 나타내는 부사절의 시제는 미래를 표현할 때 현재시제를 사용한다. 그래서 주절에는 미래의 조동사 will이 나타나 있지만, unless절에는 현재시제 practice가 쓰였다.

- even while demonstrating how powerful our subconscious really is

how 이하는 demonstrating의 목적어절로 간접의문 형태이다. 〈의문사(how powerful)+주어 (our subconscious)+동사(is)〉의 어순임에 주의한다.

GRAMMAR Quiz

1. 너는 이 방에서 떠들면 안 된다.
   → You are not to make a noise in this room.
   〈의무〉

2. 그녀는 치명적인 사고 이후 결코 걷지 못할 것이었다.
   → She was never to walk after the accident.
   〈운명〉

STRUCTURE

The person falling into a hypnotic trance speaks and possibly reveals something best left unrevealed.

○ The person이란 어떤 사람을 말하는가?
   → falling into a hypnotic trance
   → 해석: 최면 상태에 빠진 사람

○ something이란 어떤 것인가?
   → best left unrevealed
   → 해석: 밝혀지지 않은 채 남아 있는 것이 최선인 것

〈문장의 구조〉
- 주어 → The person falling into a hypnotic trance
- 동사 → speaks and possibly reveals
- 목적어 → something best left unrevealed

WRITING

1. The magician asks a member of the audience to join him on stage for his next trick, hypnotizing someone so that he or she will do something funny.
   (그 또는 그녀가 재미있는 무언가를 할 수 있도록)

2. It can be used to control our brains so that we alter our behavior. (조절하는 데에 사용될 수 있다)

3. Hypnosis is a scientific method which allows us to enter the subconscious in order to reprogram desires and effect behavior changes.
   (우리를 ~로 들어가게 하다)

4. Hypnosis has been likened to playing a musical instrument. (연주하는 것에 비유되어 왔다)

5. Many professionals manage to make people laugh even while demonstrating how powerful our subconscious really is.
   (우리의 잠재의식이 정말 얼마나 강력한지)

Passage 14

| 정답 |

1. ③
2. 아버지의 류머티즘을 위한 약을 만들기 위해서
3. ③
4. ④

| 해설 |

1. (A), (B), (C)에 언급된 연도를 주의하여 살핀다. (B)에는 바이엘이 사망한 당시 1880년에 대한 언급이고, (C)는 그 이후 아스피린을 개발하게 된 1897년이 나오고 있다. 초기 아스피린의 부작용을 해결하게 되는 1897년 10월에 대한 (A)가 마지막에 오는 것이 가장 자연스럽다.

2. (C)의 to try to find a drug which would help his father deal with the medical condition of rheumatism에 Felix Hoffmann이 아스피린을 연구하게 된 최초 이유가 나타나 있다. 즉, '아버지의 류머티즘을 위한 약을 만들기 위해서' 였다.

3. 결론 부분으로, 바이엘 사가 아스피린과 동의어가 되었다는 내용이 가장 적절하므로, ③ synonymous with(~과 동의어인)가 정답이다.
   ① ~에 의존하는   ② ~에 영향을 미치는
   ④ 잘 사는   ⑤ 특허된

4. (C)에서 보면, ④ Aspirin was first invented by one of Bayer's scientists.(아스피린은 바이엘 사이 과학자들 중 한 명에 의해 발명되었다.)가 일치하는 내용임을 알 수 있다.
   다음 중 이 글의 내용으로 옳은 것은?
   ① 아스피린이라는 이름은 그 약의 최초 발명가에서 왔다.
   ② Friedrich Bayer은 일생을 아스피린의 발명에 바쳤다.
   ③ 아스피린 발명에 참여한 사람들이 많았다.
   ⑤ Hofmann은 무엇이 부작용을 초래했는지 이해하지 못했다.

| 본문 |

Born in 1825, Friedrich Bayer was one of six children in his family. Bayer took up his father's trade, dyeing and weaving, and started a successful dye business of his own in 1848.

After the discovery of coal-tar based dyes in 1856, Bayer and another master dyer, Friedrich Weskott, formed the Friedrich Bayer Company to manufacture such dyes since they thought such dyes had great commercial potential.

(B) When Bayer died on May 6, 1880, the company was involved principally in the fabric dye business. After Bayer's death the company continued to hire chemists to invent new dyes and other products which were based on the new dyes.

(C) In 1897, one of the Friedrich Bayer Company's chemists, Felix Hoffmann, conducted experiments with some of the various chemicals used in the dyes to try to find a drug which would help his father deal with the medical condition of rheumatism. Eventually a stable form of salicylic acid which came from the bark of the willow tree was chemically synthesized by Hoffman. The compound became the active ingredient in a pharmaceutical wonder product: Aspirin. The "a" came from acetyl, and the "spir" came from the spirea plant, which salicin comes from.

(A) While it relieved pain, the powder form of aspirin, salicylic acid, irritated the drug taker's stomach and mouth. This side effect was not solved until Hoffmann, on August 10, 1897, produced a chemically pure type of acetyl salicylic acid. The Bayer Company thus became synonymous with the drug aspirin.

| 해석 |

1825년에 태어난 Friedrich Bayer은 그 가족의 여섯 아이들 중 하나였다. Bayer은 아버지의 장사인 직물을 염색하고 짜는 일을 시작하게 되었고, 1848년에 자신의 염료 사업을 성공적으로 이끌게 되었다. 1856년 콜타르에 기초한 염료 발견 이후에, Bayer과 또 다른 염색공 대가인 Friedrich Weskott은 그러한 염료가 상업적 잠재력이 크다고 생각해서 그러한 염료들을 제조하기 위해 프리드리히 바이엘이라는 회사를 설립했다.

(B) Bayer이 1880년 5월 6일 사망했을 때, 그 회사는 주로 직물 염료 사업에 종사했었다. Bayer의 죽음 이후에, 그 회

사는 새로운 염료와 그 새로운 염료에 기초한 다른 상품들을 만들어내기 위해서 화학자들을 계속 고용했다.

(C) 1897년, 프리드리히 바이엘 회사 화학자들 중 한 명인 Felix Hoffmann은 그의 아버지가 류머티즘이라는 의학적 상태를 치료하는 데에 도움이 될 약을 찾아내기 위해서 그 염료에 쓰인 다양한 화학 성분을 가지고 실험을 했다. 결국 버드나무 껍질에서 나온 살리실산이라는 안정된 형태가 Hoffman에 의해서 화학적으로 합성되었다. 그 화합물은 제약계의 놀라운 작품인 아스피린이라는 특효 있는 성분이었다. "a"는 아세틸인 acetyl에서 왔고, "spir"는 살리신이 나오는 관목나무인 spirea에서 왔다.

(A) 그것이 통증을 가라앉히는 동안, 아스피린의 가루 형태인 살리실산은 그 약의 복용자의 위와 입에 염증을 일으켰다. 이 부작용은 1897년 8월 10일 Hoffmann이 아세틸 살리실산이라는 화학적으로 순수한 약을 만들고나서야 해결되었다. 그래서 바이엘 회사는 아스피린이라는 약과 <u>동의어</u>가 되었다.

| 구문 |

- This side effect was not solved until Hoffmann ~ produced a chemically pure type of acetyl salicylic acid.
  〈not ~ until〉 구문이며, '…까지 ~않다, …이 되어서야 비로소 (~하다)' 라고 해석한다.

- a drug which would help his father deal with the medical condition of rheumatism
  동사 help는 목적어나 목적격보어로 to부정사나 동사원형 모두 쓸 수 있다.

GRAMMAR Quiz

1. 그 책은 쉬운 영어로 쓰여 있어서, 읽기가 쉬웠다.
   → As the book is written in easy English, it is easy to read.

2. 이 꽃은 '장미' 라고 우리에 의해 불린다.
   → This flower is called 'a rose' by us.

STRUCTURE

Eventually a stable form of salicylic acid which came from the bark of the willow tree was chemically synthesized by Hoffman.

○ 살리실산(salicylic acid)은 어디서 구한 것인가?
  → came from the bark of the willow tree
  → 해석: 버드나무 껍질에서 얻은

○ Eventually가 수식하는 것은?
  → 문장 전체

〈문장의 구조〉
- (문장 부사) → Eventually
- 주어 → a stable form of salicylic acid which came from the bark of the willow tree
- 동사 → was
- 보어 → chemically synthesized
- (전치사구) → by Hoffman

WRITING

1. While it relieved pain, the powder form of aspirin, salicylic acid, irritated the drug taker's stomach and mouth.
   (그것이 통증을 가라앉히는 동안)

2. This side effect <u>was not solved until</u> Hoffmann, on August 10, 1897, produced a chemically pure type of acetyl salicylic acid.
   (~할 때까지 해결되지 않았다)

3. Felix Hoffmann <u>conducted experiments with</u> some of the various chemicals used in the dyes to try to find a drug. (~을 가지고 실험을 했다)

4. A drug <u>would help his father deal with</u> the medical condition of rheumatism.
   (그의 아버지가 ~을 치료하도록 돕다)

5. Eventually a stable form of salicylic acid which came from the bark of the willow tree <u>was chemically synthesized by</u> Hoffman.
   (~에 의해서 화학적으로 합성되었다)

Passage

| 정답 |

1. ⑤
2. ③
3. 그 모양이 매우 다양하고 복잡하다.
4. 상대적으로 젊은 성운이다. / 매우 작은 성운이다. / 질소 가스로 둘러싸여 있다.

| 해설 |

1. 성운은 행성처럼 보이지만, 사실은 가스 구름으로 행성과는 상관이 없다. 그러므로 빈칸에는 ⑤ But, in fact, the planetary nebula has nothing to do with planets.(그러나 사실 성운은 행성과는 관련이 없다.)가 가장 적절하다.
   ① 그래서 성운이라는 이름은 단지 몇몇 사람들 사이에서만 사용되었다.
   ② 그러나 성운은 최근 이미지들의 이름을 따서 이름이 다시 지어졌다.
   ③ 그러나 성운이라는 이름은 18세기에는 주어지지 않았다.
   ④ 성운이라는 이름이 나타내듯이, 그것은 행성의 형태이다.

2. 성운은 별이 그 일생의 마지막 단계에서 일어나는 현상이다. 그러므로 모여서 별이 된다는 ③ They gather together and eventually become big enough to form a star.(성운은 모여서 별을 형성할 만큼 충분히 커진다.)는 사실이 아니다.
   다음 중 성운에 관한 사실이 아닌 것은?
   ① 성운은 별의 일생의 마지막에 형성되는 별의 외곽이 타는 가스이다.
   ② 그 이름은 다른 행성들의 모습과 비슷하다는 데에서 비롯되었다.
   ④ 기술이 좋아진 망원경이 성운이 복잡하고 다양한 모양이라는 것을 밝혀냈다.
   ⑤ 성운은 만 년 이상 지속되는 상대적으로 짧은 수명을 가지는 현상이다.

3. nebulae are actually like snowflakes, showing an incredibly diverse and complex range of shapes에서 답을 알 수 있다. 즉, snowflakes와 planetary nebulae은 그 모양이 매우 다양하고 복잡하다는 점에서 서로 비슷하다.

4. The relatively youthful nebula is quite small and is surrounded by nitrogen gas. Nitrogen produces red light.에서 정답을 찾아볼 수 있다. 붉은빛을 내는 planetary nebula는 상대적으로 젊고, 매우 작으며 질소 가스로 둘러싸여 있는 성운이다.

| 본문 |

As stars burn out they emit glowing gases, which make colorful and complex shapes when viewed by powerful telescopes such as the Hubble Space Telescope. These emissions or gaseous clouds are known as planetary nebulae. Originally viewed in the eighteenth century through small and less powerful telescopes, astronomers thought the round shape of these gaseous clouds looked like the other planets in the solar system. But, in fact, the planetary nebula has nothing to do with planets.

Planetary nebulae are produced when stars in their final stages of life shed their top layers of material. This material turns into gaseous clouds which are illuminated by ultraviolet light from the remnant star. These glowing gaseous clouds last for about a few tens of thousands of years, which is not a long time considering such sun-like stars usually have a lifespan of over 10 billion years. As time passes these gaseous clouds expand and become larger. Furthermore, as time passes the ultraviolet light penetrates more deeply into the gas, causing the nebulae to glow more brightly.

Modern images of planetary nebulae show how they expand and contract in varied size as well as in temperature. In terms of their shape, nebulae are actually like snowflakes, showing an incredibly diverse and complex range of shapes. The relatively youthful nebula is quite small and is surrounded by nitrogen gas. Each color represents a different kind of gas being emitted. Nitrogen produces red light; hydrogen produces green light; and oxygen produces blue light.

| 해석 |

별은 타오를 때, 빨갛게 타오르는 가스를 발산하는데, 허블 우주 망원경 같은 강력한 망원경으로 보면 그 가스는 색채가 다양하고 복잡한 모양을 만들어낸다. 이러한 발산, 즉 가스 구름은 성운이라 알려져 있다. 18세기에 작고 덜 강력한 망원경으로 처음 관찰했을 때, 천문학자들은 이러한 성운의 둥근 모양이 태양계의 다른 행성처럼 보인다고 생각했다. 그러나 사실 성운은 행성과 관련이 없다.

성운은 별이 그 일생의 마지막 단계에서 최외곽층 물질을 발산할 때 생성된다. 이 물질은 별의 잔존물에서 나오는 자외선으로 광채를 더하는 가스 구름으로 변한다. 이렇게 타오르는 성운은 거의 수만 년 동안 지속되는데, 태양과 같은 별이 보통 100억 년 이상의 수명을 가지고 있다는 것을 고려하면 긴 시간은 아니다. 시간이 지남에 따라, 성운은 팽창하고 더욱 커진다. 게다가, 시간이 지남에 따라 자외선은 그 기체 속으로 더욱 깊이 침투해서, 성운이 더 밝게 타오르게 한다.

성운의 현대식 이미지들은 성운이 어떻게 다양한 기온뿐 아니라 다양한 크기로 팽창하고 수축하는지를 보여 준다. 그 모양으로 보면, 성운은 실제로 눈꽃송이와 같아서 굉장히 다양하고 복잡한 모양을 보여 준다. 상대적으로 젊은 성운은 상당히 작고, 질소 가스로 둘러싸여 있다. 각각의 색깔은 다른 종류의 가스가 발산된다는 것을 나타낸다. 질소는 붉은빛을, 수소는 초록빛을, 산소는 푸른빛을 생성한다.

| 구문 |

• they emit glowing gases, which make colorful and complex shapes
여기서 which는 glowing gases를 받는 관계대명사의 계속적 용법으로 쓰였다.

GRAMMAR Quiz

1. As I have read the newspaper, I know about the accident.
   → Having read the newspaper, I know about the accident.

2. As it was fine, we went on a picnic.
   → It being fine, we went on a picnic.

STRUCTURE

These glowing gaseous clouds last for about a few tens of thousands of years, which is not a long time considering such sun-like stars usually have a lifespan of over 10 billion years.

◯ which의 선행사는?
   → a few tens of thousands of years

◯ considering 다음에 생략된 말을 쓰고, 이를 if절로 바꾸어 쓰시오.
   → considering (that)
   → if you consider that
   → 해석: (당신이) ~을 고려해 본다면

〈문장의 구조〉

• 주어   → These glowing gaseous clouds
• 동사   → last
• (전치사구)   → for about a few tens of thousands of years
• (관계사절)   → , which is not a long time
• (분사구)   → considering such sun-like stars usually have a lifespan of over 10 billion years

WRITING

1. The planetary nebula has nothing to do with planets. (~과 관련이 없다)

2. These glowing gaseous clouds last for about a few tens of thousands of years. (~동안 지속된다)

3. It is not a long time considering such sun-like stars usually have a lifespan of over 10 billion years. (~을 고려하면 긴 시간은 아니다)

4. As time passes the ultraviolet light penetrates more deeply into the gas, causing the nebulae to glow more brightly.
   (그 성운을 더 밝게 타오르게 하면서)

5. In terms of their shape, nebulae are actually like snowflakes, showing an incredibly diverse and complex range of shapes. (그것들의 모양으로 보면)

16

Passage

| 정답 |

1. ② / ④
2. many / many / many / a few
3. ②
4. 이 이상 현상과 관련 있는 다른 요소들이 있는가? /
   IAPV가 어떻게 미국으로 건너왔는가?

| 해설 |

1. ② The virus has been found in imported bees and bee products.(그 바이러스는 수입된 꿀벌들과 벌들의 산물에서 발견되어 왔다.)와 ④ Scientists have found a reasonable solution for the bee decline.(과학자들은 꿀벌 감소에 대한 적절한 해결방법을 찾아냈다.)는 언급되어 있지 않다.
   다음 중 꿀벌의 감소에 대해 사실이 아닌 것은? (2개)
   ① 과학자들은 IAPV가 (꿀벌 수) 감소의 유일한 이유가 아닐 수도 있다고 생각한다.
   ③ 과학자들은 처음에는 두 가지 종류의 균류가 그 원인이라고 의심했다.
   ⑤ 미국에서 꿀벌의 수가 엄청나게 줄어들었다.

2. but then they discovered that these fungi were prevalent in not only the colonies experiencing Colony Collapse Disorder but also colonies which were not experiencing this disorder에서 fungi는 그런 증상이 있는 벌통과 그런 증상이 없는 벌통 모두에 많았다(many)는 것을 알 수 있다. 반면에, The IAPV virus, however, showed up in 83 percent of the colonies experiencing Colony Collapse Disorder. Only 5 percent of the colonies not experiencing this disorder had the presence of this virus in their colonies.에서 IAPV는 증상이 있는 벌통에는 많고(many) 증상이 없는 벌통에는 조금 있다(a few)는 것을 알 수 있다.

3. 꿀벌들이 사라지는 현상은 아직 원인도 확실하게 밝혀지지 않은 단계이므로, ② The case is not completely concluded yet.(문제는 아직 완전하게 해결되지 않았다.)를 추론할 수 있다.
   다음 중 이 글에서 추론할 수 있는 것은?

① 다른 나라에서 꿀벌들을 들여오는 것은 금지될 것이다.
③ 미국에서 꿀벌의 개체수는 다시 증가할 것이다.
④ 과학자들은 그 바이러스를 없애는 방법을 찾아낼 것이다.
⑤ 꿀벌 감소에 대한 연구는 2004년에 시작되었다.

4. Scientists ~, so they are continuing their research to try to find out what other factors might be involved in this process.에서 '이 이상 현상과 관련 있는 다른 요소들이 있는지'에 대해 계속 연구하고 있다는 것을 알 수 있다. 또한 They also want to find out how IAPV came to the United States.에서 'IAPV가 어떻게 미국으로 건너왔는지'에 대한 연구도 진행되고 있으리라는 것을 알 수 있다.

| 본문 |

Honeybees are disappearing for unknown reasons around the United States. The decline has been drastic: In 2006, 23 percent of honeybees kept by beekeepers disappeared. Scientists are trying to come up with a possible explanation for the bee decline, also called Colony Collapse Disorder. Scientists first looked for evidence of microbes living only in the sick colonies. Two types of fungi were suspected of causing Colony Collapse Disorder. And another suspect was a little-known virus called Israeli Acute Paralysis Virus (IAPV).

Researchers have been studying bee colonies in which the bees have been disappearing and comparing those colonies to colonies in which the bees have not been disappearing. At first researchers thought the prime suspects were two types of fungi, but then they discovered that these fungi were prevalent in not only the colonies experiencing Colony Collapse Disorder but also colonies which were not experiencing this disorder.

The IAPV virus, however, showed up in 83 percent of the colonies experiencing Colony Collapse Disorder. Only 5 percent of the colonies not experiencing this disorder had the presence of this virus in their colonies. In 2004, researchers in Israel first claimed that the virus kills bees. But until now, bee experts haven't paid much attention to it. But they now know that the presence of IAPV is a strong sign that a colony has the disorder. Scientists are not sure whether IAPV can single-handedly cause Colony Collapse Disorder, so they are continuing their research to try to find out what other factors might be involved in this process. They also want to find out how IAPV came to the United States. Currently bee products are being imported from Canada, Australia, and New Zealand. However, if it turns out that this trade is spreading disease, the rules might eventually change.

| 해설 |

미국에서 꿀벌들이 알려지지 않은 이유로 사라지고 있다. 그 감소 정도는 심하다. 2006년에는 양봉업자들이 키우는 꿀벌의 23%가 사라졌다. 과학자들은 군집 붕괴 현상(CCD)이라고도 불리는 꿀벌들의 감소에 대한 가능한 설명을 찾아내기 위해 노력하고 있다. 처음에 과학자들은 병균에 침식된 벌통에만 사는 세균의 흔적을 찾았다. 두 가지 종류의 균류가 CCD를 일으킨다고 의심되었다. 그리고 또 다른 혐의는 이스라엘 급성 마비 바이러스(IAPV)라고 불리는 거의 알려지지 않은 바이러스였다.

연구원들은 꿀벌들이 사라진 벌통들을 연구해오고 있고, 그런 벌통들을 꿀벌들이 사라지지 않은 벌통들과 비교해오고 있다. 처음에 연구원들은 주요 원인이 두 가지 종류의 균류라고 생각했지만, 이러한 균류들은 CCD가 있었던 벌통뿐만 아니라, 이런 이상 현상을 겪지 않은 벌통에도 만연해 있다는 것을 알아냈다.

그러나 IAPV 바이러스는 CCD가 있었던 벌통의 83%에서 보였다. 이런 이상 현상은 겪지 않은 벌통의 단지 5%만이 벌통에서 이 바이러스가 존재했다. 2004년에, 이스라엘의 연구원들은 그 바이러스가 벌들을 죽인다고 처음으로 주장했다. 그러나 지금까지 벌 전문가들은 그것에 그다지 주의를 기울이지 않았다. 하지만, 이제 그들은 IAPV의 존재가 벌통에 이상 현상이 있다는 강력한 표시라는 것을 알고 있다. 과학자들은 IAPV가 단독으로 CCD를 일으킬 수 있는지 확신하지 못해서, 어떤 다른 요소들이 이 과정에 관련이 있을지 찾아내려고 노력하고 있다. 그들은 또한 IAPV가 어떻게 미국에 오게 되었는지 알아내고 싶어한다. 현재 꿀벌의 산물들이 캐나다, 오스트레일리아, 그리고 뉴질랜드에서 수입되고 있다.

그러나 이런 교역이 질병을 퍼뜨린다는 것이 증명된다면, 결국 규정이 바뀌게 될 것이다.

| 구문 |

• Scientists are not sure whether IAPV can single-handedly cause Colony Collapse Disorder / to try to find out what other factors might be involved in this process / They also want to find out how the IAPV came to the United States.
모두 간접의문문을 목적어로 취하고 있는 문장들이다. 〈의문사(whether, what, how+주어+동사)의 어순에 유의한다. 의문사가 없는 경우에는 if나 whether를 사용한다.

GRAMMAR Quiz

1. 만약 그녀를 다시 만나게 되면 나는 그녀에게 진실을 말할 것이다.
   → I will tell her the truth if I see her again.

2. 내가 다시 사회적으로 활동적인 사람이 될 수나 있을지 궁금하다.
   → I wonder if I will ever become socially active again.

STRUCTURE

Researchers have been studying bee colonies in which the bees have been disappearing and comparing those colonies to colonies in which the bees have not been disappearing.

➡ 밑줄 친 bee colonies란 어떤 colonies를 말하는가?
   → in which the bees have been disappearing

➡ comparing 앞에 생략된 말은?
   → researchers have been

➡ 밑줄 친 colonies란 어떤 colonies인가?
   → in which the bees have not been disappearing

〈문장의 구조〉

• 주어   → Researchers
• 동사   → have been studying
• 목적어 → bee colonies in which the bees have been disappearing
• 연결어 → and
• 동사   → comparing

- 목적어 → those colonies
- (전치사구) → to colonies in which the bees have not been disappearing

WRITING

1. Scientists <u>are trying to come up with</u> a possible explanation for the bee decline.
   (~을 찾아내기 위해 노력하고 있다)

2. Researchers <u>have been comparing</u> those colonies to colonies in which the bees have not been disappearing.
   (~을 비교해오고 있다)

3. Only 5 percent of the colonies <u>not experiencing this disorder</u> had the presence of this virus in their colonies. (이런 병을 겪지 않은)

4. In 2004, researchers in Israel first <u>claimed that the virus kills bees.</u>
   (그 바이러스가 벌들을 죽인다고 주장했다)

5. So they are continuing their research to try to find out <u>what other factors might be involved in this process.</u> (어떤 다른 요소들이 관련이 있을지)

Review

| A |
- 01. 다양한
- 02. 발산하다
- 03. 비추다, 광채를 더하다
- 04. 성운
- 05. 산소 (cf. hydrogen 수소)
- 06. 침투하다, 관통하다
- 07. 제약의
- 08. 우세하다, 이기다
- 09. 안정된
- 10. 잠재의식(의)
- 11. 동의어의, 같은 뜻의
- 12. 혼수상태

| B |
- 01. fall into a trance
- 02. a pharmaceutical company
- 03. emit heat, light or gas
- 04. hidden power of the subconscious
- 05. The price of oil should remain stable.
- 06. Security is synonymous with Safety.

| C |
- 01. illuminate
- 02. penetrates
- 03. oxygen
- 04. Nebula
- 05. diverse
- 06. prevails

| D |
- 01. ③
- 02. ③
- 03. ③
- 04. ②
- 05. ②
- 06. ②
- 07. ①
- 08. ①
- 09. ③
- 10. ②

Chapter 05

Vocabulary Pre-check

- affect (악)영향을 미치다
- assurance 확신
- at least 적어도
- awkwardly 서투르게, 어색하게
- bipolar 쌍극성의
- breed 번식시키다, 낳다
- capacity 능력, 용량
- cattle 소, 가축
- clinically 임상적으로
- command 명령(하다)
- composition 구성
- concentrate 집중하다
- depression 우울(증)
- diplomatic 외교의
- ecstatic 희열에 넘친, 황홀한
- estimate 어림잡다, 추정하다
- excitable 자극받기 쉬운
- extinction 멸종
- extreme 극심한
- fatal 치명적인
- figure 숫자, 모습
- get around 이겨내다, 헤어나다
- hind feet 뒷다리
- hybrid 혼혈의
- impair 손상하다, 해치다
- impressive 인상적인
- indicate 가리키다, 지적하다
- inevitably 불가피하게, 반드시
- justify 정당함을 증명하다
- lay (알을) 낳다, (~을) 놓다
- manic-depressive 조울증의
- marinated 양념된
- mating season 짝짓기 철
- membrane 세포막
- normalization 정상화
- occupy 점령하다, 차지하다, 거주하다
- outweigh ~보다 가치가 있다, 중요하다
- photographic memory 사진처럼 선명한 기억력
- possess 소유하다
- pros and cons 장단점, 찬반양론
- regarding ~에 관한
- regulator 규정자, 단속자
- reproduce 번식하다, 생식하다
- revelation 폭로, 의외의 일
- shallow 얕은
- skeptical 의심 많은, 회의적인
- spade-like 쟁기모양의
- standard 표준
- strain 긴장시키다
- sufficient 충분한
- swing 변동, 동요
- territory 영토
- unidentifiable 확인될 수 없는
- use up 다 써버리다

17

| 정답 |

1. ④
2. S. multiplicata males / fast-developing tadpoles / they dry up
3. • pros: 빨리 성장하므로 물이 마르기 전에 살 수 있는 확률이 크다.
   • cons: 성장해서 번식을 못 하는 경향이 있다.
4. ③

| 해설 |

1. Two spadefoot species, ~, both live in the southwestern United States, where they often occupy the same territory.라는 문장으로 보아, ④ Different species of spadefoot toad can live in the same area.(쟁기발두꺼비의 서로 다른 종들은 같은 지역에서 살 수 있다.)가 글의 내용과 일치한다는 것을 알 수 있다.
   다음 중 사실인 것은?
   ① 쟁기발두꺼비들은 얕은 물에 알을 낳으려고 하지 않는다.
   ② 쟁기발두꺼비들은 엄격하게 제한된 종들과만 짝짓기를 한다.
   ③ 올챙이들은 건기 동안 육지에 살도록 적응할 것이다.
   ⑤ 많은 쟁기발두꺼비들이 멸종의 위협에 직면해 있다.

2. 본문의 내용을 요약하면 다음과 같을 것이다.
   → S. bombifrons females will break the usual rule and mate with S. multiplicata males in order to produce fast-developing tadpoles that will hop out of those shallow pools before they dry up.
   (S. bombifrons 암컷은 얕은 웅덩이가 말라버리기 전에 올챙이들이 빠져나오도록 빠르게 성장하는 올챙이를 낳기 위해 일반적인 규칙을 깨고 S. multiplicata 수컷과 짝짓기를 할 것이다.)

3. 서로 다른 종들이 짝짓기를 하는 장점은 혼혈 올챙이가 더 빨리 성장해서 물이 마르기 전에 살 수 있는 확률이 크다는 것이고, 단점은 성장해서 번식을 못 하는 경향이 있다는 것이다.

4. occupy는 「점령하다, 차지하다, 거주하다」라는 의미이므로 ③ inhabit와 같다.

| 본문 |

Since it lives in the dry hot desert, the Spadefoot Toad, which has long, pointy spade-like hind feet, has been forced to adapt for its survival. The dry weather causes special problems during the mating season. Females lay their eggs in pools of water, but if the pools dry up before the tadpoles become toads, the Spadefoot Toad might face extinction since tadpoles cannot live on dry land as toads can.

A new study shows that spadefoot parents get around this problem in a very unusual way. Most animal species don't breed with one another, and spadefoots generally don't either. But they will during dry seasons if it helps their young survive. Two spadefoot species, Spea bombifrons and Spea multiplicata, both live in the southwestern United States, where they often occupy the same territory. They can mate with each other, though there are pros and cons to doing so.

On the one side for S. bombifrons, the hybrid tadpoles develop faster than tadpoles with two S. bombifrons parents. The hybrid tadpoles are therefore more likely to survive if they are born in a shallow pool that dries up quickly. On the other side, the hybrids tend to have problems reproducing once they become adults. Scientists have discovered that when S. bombifrons females are breeding in particularly shallow pools, they seem to decide that the pros of breeding with the other species outweigh the cons.

| 해석 |

길고 뾰족한 쟁기모양의 뒷다리를 가진 쟁기발두꺼비는 건조하고 뜨거운 사막에 살기 때문에, 그 생존에 적합하도록 (환경에) 적응해 왔다. 건조한 날씨는 짝짓기 철에 특별한 문제를 일으킨다. 암컷은 물 웅덩이에 알을 낳는데, 올챙이가 두꺼비가 되기 전에 웅덩이가 말라버리면, 올챙이는 두꺼비처럼 건조한 육지에서는 살 수 없기 때문에, 그 쟁기발두꺼비는 멸종에 직면하게 될지도 모른다.

새로운 연구는 쟁기발 두꺼비 부모는 매우 특이한 방법으로 이 문제를 이겨낸다는 것을 보여 준다. 대부분의 동물들은 서로 함께 번식시키지 않고, 쟁기발들도 일반적으로는 그렇지 않다. 그러나 건기 동안에는 그것이 어린 것들을 살아남게 하는 데에 도움이 된다면, 그것들은 그렇게 할 것이다. Spea bombifrons and Spea multiplicata라는 두 마리의 쟁기발 종은 미국 남서부에 함께 사는데, 거기에서 그것들은 종종 같은 영토를 점령하고 있다. 그렇게 하는 데 대해 장단점이 있지만, 그것들은 서로 짝짓기를 할 수 있다.

S. bombifrons 측에서는, 그 혼혈 올챙이들은 부모가 둘 다 S. bombifrons인 올챙이들보다 더 빠르게 성장한다. 그래서 혼혈 올챙이들은 빠르게 말라버리는 얕은 웅덩이에서 태어나도, 살아남을 가능성이 더 높다. 이와는 달리, 혼혈종들은 어른이 되면 번식하는 데에 문제를 가지게 되는 경향이 있다. 과학자들은 S. bombifrons 암컷이 특별히 얕은 웅덩이에 알을 낳을 때, 다른 종들과 번식하는 이로움이 단점보다 가치가 있다고 결정하는 것 같다는 것을 발견했다.

| 구문 |

- tadpoles cannot live on dry land like toads can (live on dry land) / Most animal species don't breed with one another, and spadefoots generally don't either (breed with one another).
  영어에서는 반복되는 부분을 생략하는 경우가 많다. 앞의 문장에서는 can 뒤에 live on dry land가, 뒤의 문장에서는 either 뒤에 breed with one another가 생략된 것으로 볼 수 있다.

GRAMMAR Quiz

1. You're lying to me.
2. The dog was lying on the ground.
3. I saw the book laid on the table.
4. The great ocean of truth lay undiscovered before me.

STRUCTURE

Two spadefoot species, Spea bombifrons and Spea multiplicata, both live in the southwestern United States, where they often occupy the same territory.

�𝗢 Two spadefoot species와 동격인 것은?
  → Spea bombifrons and Spea multiplicata

�𝗢 where의 선행사는?
  → in the southwestern United States

〈문장의 구조〉

- 주어 → Two spadefoot species, Spea bombifrons and Spea multiplicata, both
- 동사 → live
- (전치사구) → in the southwestern United States
- (관계부사절) → where they often occupy the same territory

WRITING

1. The Spadefoot Toad might face extinction since tadpoles cannot live on dry land as toads can.
   (두꺼비가 그럴 수 있는 것처럼)

2. Spadefoot parents get around this problem in a very unusual way. (이 문제를 이겨낸다)

3. They will during dry seasons if it helps their young survive.
   (그것이 어린 것들을 살아남게 하는 데에 도움이 된다면)

4. The hybrid tadpoles are therefore more likely to survive if they are born in a shallow pool that dries up quickly. (그래서 더 ~하게 될 것 같다)

5. On the other side, the hybrids tend to have problems reproducing once they become adults. (번식하는 데에 문제를 가지게 되는 경향이 있다)

Passage 18

| 정답 |

1. ① / ④
2. bipolar I / bipolar I / bipolar II / bipolar II
3. ③
4. manic

| 해설 |

1. 이 글에 따르면, bipolar disorder를 I과 II로 나누어 이야기하고 있으므로 ① Bipolar disorder can be divided into two types depending on its symptoms.(쌍극성 장애는 그 증상에 따라 두 가지 형태로 구분될 수 있다.)는 옳다. 또한 bipolar I disorder의 환자들은 흥분상태와 우울상태를 번갈아 겪는다고 했으므로, ④ Patients with bipolar disorder can have uplifted moods and depression by turns.(쌍극성 장애 환자들은 흥분된 상태와 우울증을 번갈아 가며 느낄 수 있다.)도 옳다.
   이 글에 따르면, 다음 중 사실인 것은? (2개)
   ② 쌍극성 장애는 어떤 후유증도 없이 쉽게 진단되고 치료될 수 있다.
   ③ 쌍극성 장애의 증상은 통상적인 기분의 변동과 아주 유사하다.
   ⑤ 쌍극성 장애를 겪는 사람들은 항상 조증과 우울증의 기간이 같다.

2. bipolar I의 증상은 심한 흥분과 우울이 반복되거나 우울이 오래 간다는 것과 사람들과의 관계가 어렵다는 것이고, bipolar II의 증상은 흥분하는 경우는 적고 주로 우울만 계속 되며 일상생활이나 사람들과의 관계에 악영향을 미치지 않는다는 것이다.

3. 주어진 문장의 If it is known으로 보아, 알려지지 않은 내용이 앞에 와야 한다는 것을 알 수 있다. 즉, The cause for the depression might be unidentifiable. 라는 문장 뒤인 (C)의 위치가 가장 적절하다.

4. ecstatic은 「희열에 넘친, 황홀한」의 뜻이다. 본문에서 같은 의미로 사용된 단어는 manic으로 우울증과 대비되는 조증을 가리킨다.

| 본문 |

Everyone experiences mood swings at times, but some people have such extreme mood swings that they are clinically ill. These people can feel ecstatic for a few weeks about something happening to them that would merely be pleasant to someone else. Then they can shift into a severe depression, being unable to concentrate and having extremely negative thoughts about themselves. The cause for the depression might be unidentifiable. If it is known, it is clear that most people would not react this deeply to this kind of problem.

In many cases such extreme mood swings indicate that the person is suffering from one of two forms of bipolar illness. The first type of bipolar illness, bipolar I disorder, was previously called manic-depressive illness. People who suffer from this illness go through either periods of mania, extreme happiness, and then depression or simply go through only a period of mania or depression. People who are experiencing bipolar I disorder have trouble relating to others because of their disorder. To be considered to be going through an episode of depression, the period of depression must last at least two weeks, but a clinical definition of mania doesn't require that a person feel ecstatic for any set period of time.

Patients suffering from bipolar II disorder which usually starts with a depressive episode have mainly depression and a few manic episodes. They are not as socially impaired in their interactions with others as patients suffering from bipolar I disorder. They carry on in their daily life and with their daily routines.

| 해석 |

모든 사람이 때때로 기분이 바뀌는 것을 경험하지만, 어떤 사람들은 임상적으로 앓고 있는 극심한 기분의 변동을 겪는다. 이런 사람들은 다른 사람에게는 단순히 즐거울 만한 그들에게 일어나는 어떤 일들에 대해 몇 주간 흥분해 있을 수

있다. 그리고 나서 그들은 심한 우울기로 접어들어, 집중하지 못하고 스스로에 대해 극도로 부정적인 생각을 하게 될 수 있다. 이런 우울증에 대한 원인은 확인되지 않을 것이다. 알게 되다면, 대부분의 사람들은 이런 종류의 문제에 이렇게 깊이 반응하지 않을 것이 분명하다.

많은 경우 그런 극심한 기분 변동은 그 사람이 두 가지 형태의 쌍극성 장애 중 하나로 고통받고 있다는 것을 나타낸다. 쌍극성 장애의 한 형태인 bipolar I disorder는 이전에 조울증이라고 불리었다. 이 질병을 앓는 사람들은 극도의 행복을 느끼다가 그 후에는 우울증을 느끼는 조울증의 기간을 겪거나, 단순히 조증이나 우울증의 한 기간만을 겪는다. bipolar I disorder를 겪고 있는 사람들은 그들의 장애 때문에 다른 사람들과 관계를 맺는 데에 문제가 있다. 우울증의 한 시기를 겪고 있다고 여겨지기 위해서는, 우울증의 시기가 적어도 2주간 지속되어야 하지만, 조증의 임상적 정의는 어떤 사람이 어떤 기간 동안 황홀함을 느껴야 한다는 것은 필요하지 않다.

일반적으로 침울한 시기로 시작되는 bipolar II disorder로 고생하는 사람들은 주로 우울증이 있고 약간의 조증 시기가 있다. 그들은 bipolar I disorder로 고생하는 환자들만큼 다른 사람들과 상호작용을 하는 데에 있어 사회적으로 손상되지 않았다. 그들은 일상생활과 일상의 일들을 해나간다.

| 구문 |

- People who suffer from this illness / go through either periods of mania, extreme happiness, and then depression / or simply go through only a period of mania or depression.

  who는 People을 선행사로 하는 주격 관계대명사이다. 주어 People에 동사 go 두 개가 or로 연결되어 있다.

- People (who are) experiencing bipolar I disorder have ~ / Patients (who are) suffering from bipolar II disorder which usually starts with a depressive episode have ~

  People과 experiencing 사이, People과 suffering 사이에는 (who are)가 생략된 것으로 볼 수 있다. 〈주격 관계대명사+be동사〉는 생략할 수 있다는 것을 알아둔다.

Passage 19

| 정답 |

1. ②
2. ③
3. 햄버거의 쇠고기 패티를 먹으면 미치게 되지는 않는지 생각한다. / 주부들이 쇠고기의 원산지를 꼼꼼히 확인한다. / 식당의 값싼 쇠고기 양념 갈비는 미국에서 수입된 것이라고 생각한다.
4. ③ / ④

| 해설 |

1. 주어진 문장의 stress 앞의 정관사 the로 보아, 그것에 관한 내용이 앞에 있어야 한다. (B) 앞의 to strain diplomatic relationships에서 그 내용이 시작되고 있고, 사람들이 건강을 걱정하여 하는 행동들이 그 뒤에 언급되고 있으므로, 주어진 문장은 (B)에 들어가야 한다.

2. inevitably는 「불가피하게, 필연적으로, 반드시」의 의미이다. 이에 가장 가까운 단어는 ③ unavoidably이다.
   ① 마침내　　② 결국
   ④ 확실히　　⑤ 점차적으로

3. this skeptical behavior는 사람들이 광우병에 대해 불안해하는 행동들이다. 그러므로 햄버거의 쇠고기 패티를 먹으면 미치게 되지는 않는지 걱정하고, 주부들이 쇠고기의 원산지를 꼼꼼히 확인하며, 식당의 값싼 쇠고기 양념 갈비는 미국에서 수입된 것이라고 생각하는 것이다.

4. 두 번째 단락의 Scientists tell the public that by eating infected beef they can get the same disease cows have.에서 보면, ③ The disease can be transferred to a person who eats infected beef.(그 질병은 감염된 쇠고기를 먹는 사람에게 전이될 수 있다.)는 옳다. 또한 한국 사람들은 광우병에 걸린 소를 먹게 될까봐 걱정하고 있다고 했으므로, ④ Korean people became very hesitant about buying imported beef.(한국 사람들은 수입 쇠고기를 사는 것에 대해 매우 주저하게 되었다.)도 옳다는 것을 알 수 있다.
   이 글에 따르면, 다음 중 사실인 것은? (2개)
   ① 미국에 광우병에 걸린 많은 사례들이 있었다.
   ② 미국 정부는 쇠고기 수출을 정상화하는 데 성공했다.
   ⑤ 광우병은 많은 나라들에서 수입된 쇠고기에서 발견되었다.

| 본문 |

A single case of mad cow disease in December of 2003 has greatly affected the trading relationship between Korea and America. Americans have been pushing for the normalization of beef trade, but Koreans have been concerned about their health. After all, mad cow disease is fatal and public fears are not easily pushed aside by the assurances of government regulators. Defining 'normalization' is not an easy thing to do, but Korea is following international standards regarding the safety and importation of American beef these days. Nevertheless, it is clear that the revelation in December of 2003 that one American cow had mad cow disease will <u>inevitably</u> continue to strain diplomatic relationships. <u>The stress results partly from the public's fears about health.</u>

Scientists tell the public that by eating infected beef they can get the same disease cows have. So citizens cannot put a burger to their lips without wondering if the beef patty will make them go crazy. Furthermore, housewives now carefully check the origin of beef they buy in the supermarket. And people think that cheap prices for marinated beef ribs in restaurants must mean they have been imported from America. So, you ought to think twice before eating there.

The origin of <u>this skeptical behavior</u> is the horrible nature of the disease itself. Cattle infected with this disease exhibit odd and strange behavior. They seem to be constantly stressed and nervous. They fall down unexpectedly and walk awkwardly. The reason is that the animals' brain and central nervous system are being broken down by the disease. And because the disease has the same effect on humans, well, our doubts seem justified.

| 해석 |

2003년 12월에 발병된 광우병의 한 병증이 한국과 미국 사이의 무역관계에 지대한 영향을 미쳐왔다. 미국인들은 쇠고기 무역의 정상화를 끈질기게 요구해오고 있지만, 한국인들은 건강을 걱정하고 있다. 어쨌든, 광우병은 치명적이라서 정부 당국의 보증에도 불구하고 국민들의 두려움은 쉽사리 수그러들지 않는다. '정상화'의 범위를 어디까지라고 결정짓는 것은 쉬운 일이 아니지만, 한국은 최근 미국 쇠고기의 안전과 수입에 관한 국제 표준을 따르고 있다. 그럼에도 불구하고, 미국산 소 한 마리에 광우병이 있었다는 2003년 12월의 폭로(밝혀짐)는 외교 관계를 불가피하게 계속 긴장시킬 것이 분명하다. 그 긴장은 부분적으로는 건강을 걱정하는 국민들의 두려움에 기인한다.

과학자들은 대중들에게 감염된 쇠고기를 먹음으로써 소가 앓고 있는 같은 질병을 얻을 수 있다고 말한다. 그래서 시민들은 햄버거를 입에 댈 때마다 쇠고기 패티가 그들을 미치게 만들지 의심하게 된다. 더욱이 가정주부들은 이제 슈퍼에서 사는 쇠고기의 원산지를 꼼꼼하게 살핀다. 그리고 사람들은 식당의 양념 소갈비 가격이 싸면, 틀림없이 미국에서 수입된 것이라는 것을 의미한다고 생각한다. 그래서 그런 식당에서 먹기 전에 두 번 생각해야 한다.

이런 의심 많은 행동의 근원은 그 병 자체의 끔찍한 특징 때문이다. 이 질병에 감염된 소들은 기묘하고 이상한 행동을 보인다. 소들이 끊임없이 긴장하고 불안한 것처럼 보인다. 소들이 갑자기 넘어지거나 비틀거리며 걷는다. 그 이유는 그 동물의 뇌와 중심 신경 체계가 그 질병에 의해 손상되었기 때문이다. 그리고 그 질병이 인간에게 같은 영향을 미치기 때문에, 우리가 염려하는 것도 납득할 만하다.

| 구문 |

• it is clear that the revelation (in December of 2003) [that one American cow had mad cow disease] will inevitably continue to strain diplomatic relationships

it is clear that ~의 that은 진주어 that절이며, that one American cow had mad cow disease의 that은 the revelation과 동격을 나타내는 that이다.

• So citizens cannot put a burger to their lips without wondering if the beef patty will make them go crazy.

〈not ~ without doing〉은 '~하면 반드시 …하다'라는 의미이다. ex. They never meet without quarreling. 그들은 만나기만 하면 반드시 싸운다.

GRAMMAR Quiz

1. 내 방에는 가구가 거의 없다.
   → I have little furniture in my room.

2. 성직자들은 그 회의에 참석했다.
   → The clergy were present at the meeting.

3. 가금류는 사람이 먹을 식량으로 고기와 달걀을 제공하기 위해 사육되는 조류이다.
   → Poultry are birds that are raised to provide meat and eggs for human food.

STRUCTURE

The revelation in December of 2003 that one American cow had mad cow disease will inevitably continue to strain diplomatic relationships.

◐ The revelation이란 어떤 내용인가?
   → 어떤 내용: that one American cow had mad cow disease
   → 해석: 미국산 쇠고기 한 마리가 광우병이 있었다는 폭로(밝혀짐)

〈문장의 구조〉
• 주어   → The revelation
• (전치사구)   → in December of 2003
• (동격절)   → that one American cow had mad cow disease
• 동사   → will inevitably continue
• 목적어   → to strain diplomatic relationships

WRITING

1. Americans have been pushing for the normalization of the beef trade.
   (~을 끈질기게 요구해오고 있다)

2. Defining 'normalization' is not an easy thing to do. (하기 쉬운 일이 아니다)

3. Scientists tell the public that by eating infected beef they can get the same disease cows have.
   (소가 지닌 같은 질병을 얻을 수 있다)

4. Citizens cannot put a burger to their lips without wondering if the beef patty will make them go crazy. (~을 의심하지 않고서는)

5. The reason is that the animals' brain and central nervous system are being broken down by the disease. (그 이유는 ~라는 것이다)

| 정답 |

1. ② / ⑤
2. ③
3. 10^{15} bits
4. ④

| 해설 |

1. The pulses ~ the neuron are commands sent by the brain telling different parts of the body what to do라는 부분에서 ② They are cells that process and transmit information.(뉴런은 정보를 처리하고 전송하는 세포이다.)의 내용을 확인할 수 있다. 또한 they are actually creating sufficient electricity에서 ⑤ They create electric pulses that travel through our body.(뉴런은 우리 몸을 통해서 이동하는 전기펄스를 만들어낸다.)의 내용도 확인해 볼 수 있다.
   다음 중 뉴런에 관해 사실인 것은? (2개)
   ① 뉴런은 신체의 각 부분에 하는 명령이다.
   ③ 뉴런은 집을 가동시킬 만큼 충분한 전기를 생성한다.
   ④ 뉴런은 인간의 신체 각 부분에서 발견될 수 있다.

2. 인간의 두뇌를 컴퓨터 용량의 10^{15} bit로 표현하면서, 언젠가 컴퓨터가 그 정도로 될 수는 있겠지만, 그렇더라도 컴퓨터가 지닐 수 없는 창조적 사고와 감정의 극도로 복잡한 과정을 언급한 이유는 ③ to imply that it is impossible for computers to surpass human brains(컴퓨터가 인간의 두뇌를 능가하는 것은 불가능하다는 것을 암시하기 위해)일 것이다.
   필자가 2번째 단락에서 인간의 창조적인 사고와 감정을 언급한 이유는 무엇인가?
   ① 컴퓨터가 나중에 (바로) 생각하고 감정을 나타낼 수 있을 것이라고 암시하기 위해
   ② 왜 컴퓨터가 인간의 두뇌와 종종 비교되는지를 설명하기 위해
   ④ 진보된 기술의 미래 목표가 무엇인지 지적하기 위해
   ⑤ 두뇌의 능력을 고려해 볼 때 무엇이 가장 중요하지 보여 주기 위해

3. 10 to the power of 15 bits은 10^{15} bits이다. 그 뒤의 petabit으로도 유추할 수 있다. 여기서 peta란 10^{15}을 의미한다.

4. (a) 언젠가 컴퓨터가 인간의 두뇌 용량과 비슷해질 수는 있겠지만, 그렇더라도 컴퓨터는 창조적 사고와 감정을 가질 수 없다는 앞뒤 문맥이므로 However가 적절하다. (b) 앞의 내용을 다시 한 번 반복하고 있으므로, In other words가 적절하다.

| 본문 |

The human brain is composed of more than 100 billion neurons (nerve cells) through which electric pulses travel at more 400 km an hour. The pulses generated by the electrically excitable membrane of the neuron are commands sent by the brain telling different parts of the body what to do. As these electric pulses travel throughout our body they are actually creating sufficient electricity to power a light bulb. The production of electricity obviously requires a fuel source which in this case is the food we eat. The brain is a huge consumer of caloric energy, using up an impressive 20% of the calories we eat.

Not only is the brain's composition special, but so is its capacity. It is estimated that the mental capacity of a 100-year old human with perfect memory could be represented by a computer with 10 to the power of 15 bits (one petabit). At the current rate of computer chip development, that figure can be reached in about 35 years. However, that represents just memory capacity, not the extremely complex processes of thought creation and emotions.

It is often thought that only a few special people possess photographic memory, but this is not true. According to scientists, anyone can train his or her brain so that he or she has 'photographic memory.' Orangutans and dolphins like humans can recognize themselves in a mirror, but only humans seem to quickly forget what they look like once they turn away from a mirror. Can you draw a picture of yourself without looking in a mirror? A few people can do this by training the brain. In other words, our capacity to memorize is not something we are born with. We need to train our brains in order to use this capacity.

| 해석 |

인간의 두뇌는 천억 개 이상의 뉴런(신경 세포)으로 구성되어 있는데, 뉴런을 통해서 전기펄스가 시속 약 400km 이상으로 이동한다. 뉴런의 전기적으로 자극받기 쉬운 세포막에 의해 생성된 펄스는 신체의 각 부분에게 무엇을 해야 할지 말해 주는 두뇌에 의해 보내지는 명령어다. 이런 전기펄스는 우리 몸 전체를 흐르면서, 실제로 작은 전구를 켤 수 있을 만큼의 충분한 전기를 만들어낸다. 전기 생산에는 분명히 연료 공급이 필요하고 이 경우에는 우리가 먹는 음식이 연료라고 할 수 있다. 두뇌는 칼로리 에너지의 막대한 소비원이어서, 우리가 섭취하는 칼로리의 20%나 되는 놀라울 정도의 많은 양을 소비한다.

두뇌는 구성이 특별할 뿐만 아니라, 그 능력도 그러하다. 완벽한 기억력을 가진 100살 노인의 정신적 능력은 컴퓨터로는 10^{15} bits로 표현될 수 있을 것이다. 컴퓨터칩 발달의 현재 속도라면, 그 숫자는 35년 정도 있으면 도달될 수 있다. 하지만, 그것은 단순한 기억 능력만을 나타내는 것이고, 창조적 사고와 감정의 극도로 복잡한 과정을 나타내는 것이 아니다.

단지 소수의 특별한 사람들만이 사진으로 찍은 것처럼 선명한 기억력을 가지고 있다고 종종 생각되고 있지만, 이것은 사실이 아니다. 과학자들에 의하면, 누구나 훈련만 하면 '사진 같은 선명한 기억력'을 가질 수 있다. 인간처럼 오랑우탄과 돌고래는 거울에서 스스로를 인식할 수 있지만, 인간만이 거울을 닫자마자 자기들이 어떻게 생겼는지를 금방 까먹는 것 같다. 거울 속을 들여다보지 않고, 스스로의 그림을 그릴 수 있는가? 두뇌를 훈련한 소수의 사람들은 그럴 수 있다. 다른 말로 하면, 기억하는 능력은 가지고 태어나는 어떤 것이 아니다. 이 능력을 사용하기 위해서는 우리 뇌를 훈련시킬 필요가 있다.

| 구문 |

• the brain telling different parts of the body what to do
동사 tell은 간접목적어(parts of the body)와 직접목적어 (what to do)를 취할 수 있다.

GRAMMAR Quiz

1. A: 너 매우 기쁜 것 같구나. — B: 정말 그래요.
   → A: You look very happy. — B: So I am.

2. A: 지난 여름에 나는 파리에 있었다. — B: 나도 그랬어.
   → A: I was in Paris last summer. — B: So was I.

STRUCTURE

The pulses generated by the electrically excitable membrane of the neuron are commands sent by the brain telling different parts of the body what to do.

○ The pulses란 어떤 전파를 이야기하는가?
   → generated by the electrically excitable membrane of the neuron

○ commands란 어떤 명령을 말하는가?
   → sent by the brain telling different parts of the body what to do

〈문장의 구조〉
• 주어 → The pulses generated by the electrically excitable membrane of the neuron
• 동사 → are
• 보어 → commands
• (분사구) → sent by the brain
• (분사구) → telling different parts of the body what to do

WRITING

1. The human brain is composed of more than 100 billion neurons through which electric pulses travel at more 400 km an hour.
   (뉴런을 통해서 전기펄스가 이동한다)

2. These electric pulses are actually creating sufficient electricity to power a light bulb.
   (전구 하나를 켤 수 있는)

3. Not only is the brain's composition special, but so is its capacity.
   (두뇌의 구성이 특별할 뿐만 아니라)

4. But only humans seem to quickly forget what they look like once they turn away from a mirror.
   (그들이 어떻게 생겼는지를)

5. Our capacity to memorize is not something we are born with. (우리가 가지고 태어나는 어떤 것)

Review

| A |

01. 적합하다, 적응하다
02. 소, 가축
03. 집중하다
04. 외교의
05. 극심한
06. 치명적인
07. (알을) 낳다, (~을) 놓다
08. 의심 많은, 회의적인
09. 충분한
10. 올챙이
11. 영토
12. 다 써버리다

| B |

01. extreme poverty
02. a herd of cattle
03. a fatal disease
04. use up all the money
05. establish diplomatic relations
06. My bird laid an egg.

| C |

01. skeptical
02. Tadpoles
03. Territory
04. sufficient
05. concentrate
06. adapt

| D |

01. ③
02. ③
03. ②
04. ①
05. ②
06. ①
07. ②
08. ②
09. ②
10. ③

상위권을 위한 필독서

AIM HIGH READING

★ **실질적인 지문과 다양한 주제** _Authentic and Various Topics

★ **독해력 향상을 위한 9가지 문제 형식** _Questions for Reading Skill Building

★ **독해력과 직결된 9가지 핵심 문법 정리** _Grammar for Reading

★ **독해력을 위한 8가지 핵심 구조 파악** _Structure for Reading

★ **독해 지문을 활용한 영작** _Writing for Reading

상위권을 위한 필독서!
AIM HIGH READING

Level 1-A · B

Level 1-A

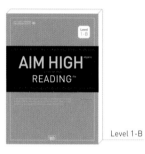

Level 1-B

- 지문 수 _ 40 (A: 20 / B: 20)
- 지문별 글자 수 _ 150~200
- 학습 기간 _ 각각 1개월 (총 2개월)
- 특징 _ 정보 스캔 및 글의 흐름 파악 문제 다수

Level 2-A · B

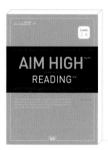

Level 2-A

Level 2-B

- 지문 수 _ 40 (A: 20 / B: 20)
- 지문별 글자 수 _ 170~220
- 학습 기간 _ 각각 1개월 (총 2개월)
- 특징 _ 세부 사항 및 어법 문제 다수

Level 3-A · B

Level 3-A

Level 3-B

- 지문 수 _ 40 (A: 20 / B: 20)
- 지문별 글자 수 _ 200~250
- 학습 기간 _ 각각 1개월 (총 2개월)
- 특징 _ 정보 스캔 및 분석 문제 다수